Thank you for choosing Desert Rose! I am honored to be a part of your journey.

IT CAN BE DONE

POEMS OF INSPIRATION

Originally collected by Joseph Morris
And St. Clair Adams

New Edition
by
Steve Morgan

*Love + godspeed!
Cynthiashmòrgan*

Double™
MOON

DoubleMoon Publishing
Lawrence, Kansas 2000

Published by DoubleMoon Publishing ™
P.O. Box 4198
Lawrence, Kansas 66046

DoubleMoonPub@aol.com

Library of Congress Control Number: 00-131816
ISBN 0-9679393-0-5

Printed by Ag Press
Manhattan, Kansas

New Introduction

My grandfather, Carl Axel Polson, a Swedish immigrant who settled in Kansas, gave me this book of poems when I was a youngster. On the inside cover, I wrote my name and the date, "January 2, 1961, NASA" (which stands for Naval Air Station in Alameda California), where I was stationed as a U.S. Navy hospital corpsman. He had given it to me before then, but I don't remember when exactly. I do remember that I prized the book for the uplift it gave me during those turbulent growing-up times. Over the years, whenever I needed its comfort, the book jumped out, saying "Read me!"

First published on November 22, 1921, it became a very popular book in a short time. My grandfather gave me the 24th edition published in June 1926. I don't know how many more editions were published.

As my daughter, Cynthia Selene Morgan, grew to young adulthood, I passed the book to her. It was, she said, a great inspiration for her. That got me to thinking. I knew the poems were old, some a lot older than the book. Some very famous poets are in the book, including the likes of Shakespeare, Tennyson, Browning, Wordsworth, Keats, Longfellow, Burns, Byron, Emerson. But many are poets not highly thought of in literary circles, though a number of them did have a popular following. One thing common to all is that they have positive, uplifting messages, something sorely missing from most of what passes for literature today. And they are highly readable. You don't need a college degree in literature to enjoy them. So, I thought, if they can inspire my daughter and me, then they can still inspire others. That's when I decided to republish the book.

I made some changes, including adding one poem and deleting 10 poems from the book that were too far removed in themes and attitudes from modern life or in a hard-to-read dialect. Some words had archaic spelling, which I modernized, except, of course, when they were part of the poetry. I changed the order of several poems, and I added additional information here and there.

May this book be as inspirational to you as it was for me.

Steve Morgan
Manhattan, Kansas
June 2000

Original Introduction

This is a volume of inspirational poems. Its purpose is to bring men courage and resolution, to cheer them, to fire them with new confidence when they grow dispirited, to strengthen their faith that THINGS CAN BE DONE. It is better for this purpose than the entire works of any one poet, for it takes the cream of many and has greater diversity than any one writer can show.

It is made up chiefly of very recent poems—not such as were written for anthologies of poetical "gems" but such as speak directly to the heart, always in very simple language, often in the phrases of shop or office or street. Included, however, with the poems of the day are a few of the fine old pieces that have been of comfort to men through the ages.

Besides the poems themselves, the volume contains helps to their understanding and enjoyment. The pieces are introduced by short comments; these serve the same purpose as the strain played by the pianist before the singer begins to sing; they create a mood, give a point of view, throw light on the meaning of what follows. Also the lives of the authors are briefly summarized; this is in answer to our natural interest in the writer of a poem we like and in the case of living poets it brings together facts hardly to be found anywhere else.

Finally, the book is not one to be read and then cast aside. It is to be kept as a constant companion and an unfailing recourse in weariness and gloom. Human companions are not always in the mood to cheer us and may talk upon themes we dislike. But this book will converse or be silent, it is never out of sorts or discouraged, and so far from being wed to some single topic, it will speak to us at any time on any subject we desire.

CONTENTS

iii

IT CAN BE DONE!

SUCCESS

As necessity is the mother of invention, strong desire is the mother of attainment.

IF you want a thing bad enough
To go out and fight for it,
Work day and night for it,
Give up your time and your peace and your sleep for it,
If only desire of it
Makes you quite mad enough never to tire of it,
Makes you hold all other things tawdry and cheap for it,
If life seems all empty and useless without it
And all that you scheme and you dream is about it,
If gladly you'll sweat for it,
Fret for it,
Plan for it,
Lose all your terror of God or man for it,
If you'll simply go after that thing that you want,
With all your capacity,
Strength and sagacity,
Faith, hope and confidence, stern pertinacity,
If neither cold poverty, famished and gaunt,
Nor sickness nor pain
Of body or brain
Can turn you away from the thing that you want,
If dogged and grim you besiege and beset it,
You'll get it!

Berton Braley

BE THE BEST OF WHATEVER YOU ARE

We all dream of great deeds and high positions, away from the pettiness and humdrum of ordinary life. Yet success is not occupying a lofty place or doing conspicuous work; it is being the best that is in you. Rattling around in too big a job is much worse than filling a small one to overflowing. Dream, aspire by all means; but do not ruin the life you must lead by dreaming pipe-dreams of the one you would like to lead. Make the most of what you have and are. Perhaps your trivial, immediate task is your one and sure way of proving your mettle. Do the thing near at hand, and great things will come to your hand to be done.

IF you can't be a pine on the top of the hill
    Be a scrub in the valley—but be
The best little scrub by the side of the rill;
    Be a bush if you can't be a tree.

If you can't be a bush be a bit of the grass,
    And some highway some happier make;
If you can't be a muskie then just be a bass—
    But the liveliest bass in the lake!

We can't all be captains, we've got to be crew,
    There's something for all of us here.
There's big work to do and there's lesser to do,
    And the task we must do is the near.

If you can't be a highway then just be a trail,
    If you can't be the sun be a star;
It isn't by size that you win or you fail—
    Be the best of whatever you are!

Douglas Malloch

IT COULDN'T BE DONE

After a thing has been done, everybody is ready to declare it easy. But before it has been done, it is called impossible. One reason why people fear to embark upon great enterprises is that they see all the difficulties at once. They know they could succeed in the initial tasks, but they shrink from what is to follow. Yet "a thing begun is half done." Moreover the surmounting of the first barrier gives strength and ingenuity for the harder ones beyond. Mountains viewed from a distance seem to be unscalable. But they can be climbed, and the way to begin is to take the first upward step. From that moment the mountains are less high. As Hannibal led his army across the foothills, then among the upper ranges, and finally over the loftiest peaks and passes of the Alps, or as Peary pushed farther and farther into the solitudes that encompass the North Pole, so can you achieve any purpose whatsoever if you heed not the doubters, meet each problem as it arises, and keep ever with you the assurance *It Can Be Done.*

SOMEBODY said that it couldn't be done,
　But he with a chuckle replied
That "maybe it couldn't," but he would be one
　Who wouldn't say so till he'd tried.
So he buckled right in with the trace of a grin
　On his face. If he worried he hid it.
He started to sing as he tackled the thing
　That couldn't be done, and he did it.

Somebody scoffed: "Oh, you'll never do that;
　At least no one ever has done it";
But he took off his coat and he took off his hat,
　And the first thing we knew he'd begun it.
With a lift of his chin and a bit of a grin,
　Without any doubting or quiddit,
He started to sing as he tackled the thing
　That couldn't be done, and he did it.

There are thousands to tell you it cannot be done,
　There are thousands to prophesy failure;
There are thousands to point out to you one by one
　The dangers that wait to assail you.
But just buckle in with a bit of a grin,
　Just take off your coat and go to it;
Just start to sing as you tackle the thing
　That "cannot be done," and you'll do it.

Edgar A. Guest

3

THE HOUSE BY THE SIDE OF THE ROAD

This poem has as its keynote friendship and sympathy for other people. It is a paradox of life that by hoarding love and happiness we lose them, and that only by giving them away can we keep them for ourselves. The more we share, the more we possess. We of course find in other people weaknesses and sins, but our best means of curing these are through a wise and sympathetic understanding.

There are hermit souls that live withdrawn
   In the peace of their self-content;
There are souls, like stars, that dwell apart,
   In a fellowless firmament;
There are pioneer souls that blaze their paths
   Where highways never ran—
But let me live by the side of the road
   And be a friend to man.

Let me live in a house by the side of the road,
   Where the race of men go by—
The men who are good and the men who are bad,
   As good and as bad as I.
I would not sit in the scorner's seat,
   Or hurl the cynic's ban—
Let me live in a house by the side of the road
   And be a friend to man.

I see from my house by the side of the road,
   By the side of the highway of life,
The men who press with the ardor of hope,
   The men who are faint with the strife.
But I turn not away from their smiles nor their
   tears—
   Both parts of an infinite plan—
Let me live in my house by the side of the road
   And be a friend to man.

I know there are brook-gladdened meadows ahead
    And mountains of wearisome height;
And the road passes on through the long afternoon
    And stretches away to the night.
But still I rejoice when the travelers rejoice,
    And weep with the strangers that moan,
Nor live in my house by the side of the road
    Like a man who dwells alone.

Let me live in my house by the side of the road
    Where the race of men go by—
They are good, they are bad, they are weak, they are strong,
    Wise, foolish—so am I.
Then why should I sit in the scorner's seat
    Or hurl the cynic's ban?—
Let me live in my house by the side of the road
    And be a friend to man.

Sam Walter Foss

IF

    The central idea of this poem is that success comes from self-control and a true sense of the values of things. A man must not lose heart because of doubts or opposition, yet he must do his best to see the grounds for both. He must not be deceived into thinking either triumph or disaster final; he must use each wisely—and push on. In all things he must hold to the golden mean. If he does, he will own the world, and even better, for his personal reward he will attain the full stature of manhood.

IF you can keep your head when all about you
    Are losing theirs and blaming it on you,
If you can trust yourself when all men doubt you,
    But make allowance for their doubting too;
If you can wait and not be tired by waiting,
    Or being lied about, don't deal in lies,
Or being hated don't give way to hating,
    And yet don't look too good, not talk too wise:

If you can dream—and not make dreams your master;
   If you can think—and not make thoughts your aim.
If you can meet with Triumph and Disaster
   And treat those two imposters just the same;
If you can bear to hear the truth you've spoken
   Twisted by knaves to make a trap for fools,
Or watch the things you gave your life to, broken,
   And stoop and build 'em up with worn-out tools:

If you can make one heap of all your winnings
   And risk it on one turn of pitch-and-toss,
And lose, and start again at your beginnings
   And never breathe a word about your loss;
If you can force your heart and nerve and sinew
   To serve your turn long after they are gone,
And so hold on when there is nothing in you
   Except the Will which says to them: "Hold on!"

If you can talk with crowds and keep your virtue,
   Or walk with Kings—nor lose the common touch,
If neither foes nor loving friends can hurt you,
   If all men count with you, but none too much;
If you can fill the unforgiving minute
   With sixty seconds' worth of distance run,
Yours is the Earth and everything that's in it,
   And—which is more—you'll be a Man, my son!

                                        Rudyard Kipling

INVICTUS

Triumph in spirit over adverse conditions is the keynote of this poem of
courage undismayed. It rings with the power of the individual to guide his own
destiny.

O UT of the night that covers me,
      Black as the Pit from pole to pole,

I thank whatever gods may be
    For my unconquerable soul.

In the fell clutch of circumstance
    I have not winced nor cried aloud.
Under the bludgeonings of chance
    My head is bloody, but unbowed.

Beyond this place of wrath and tears
    Looms but the Horror of the shade,
And yet the menace of the years
    Finds, and shall find, me unafraid.

It matters not how strait the gate,
    How charged with punishments the scroll,
I am the master of my fate:
    I am the captain of my soul.

William Ernest Henley

THE WELCOME MAN

THERE'S a man in the world who is never turned down, wherever he chances to stray; he gets the glad hand in the populous town, or out where the farms make hay; he's greeted with pleasure on deserts of sand, and deep in the aisles of the woods; wherever he goes there's the welcoming hand—he's The Man Who Delivers the Goods. The failures of life sit around and complain; the gods haven't treated them right; they've lost their umbrellas whenever there's rain, and they haven't their lanterns at night; men tire of the failures who fill with their sighs the air of their own neighborhoods; there's one who is greeted with love-lighted eyes—he's The Man Who Delivers the Goods. One fellow is lazy, and watches the clock, and waits for the whistle to blow; and one has a hammer, with which he will knock, and one tells a story of woe; and one, if requested to travel a mile, will measure the perches and roods; but one does his stunt with a whistle or smile—he's The Man Who

Delivers the Goods.   One man is afraid that he'll labor too hard—the world isn't yearning for such; and one man is always alert, on his guard, lest he put in a minute too much; and one has a grouch or a temper that's bad, and one is a creature of moods; so it's hey for the joyous and rollicking lad—for the One Who Delivers the Goods!

Walt Mason

THE QUITTER

In the famous naval duel between the Bonhomme Richard and the Serapis, John Paul Jones was hailed by his adversary to know whether he struck his colors. "I have not yet begun to fight," was his answer. When the surrender took place, it was not Jone's ship that became the prize of war. Everybody admires a hard fighter—the man who takes buffets standing up and in a spirit of "Never say die" is always ready for more.

WHEN you're lost in the wild and you're scared as a
    child,
    And death looks you bang in the eye;
And you're sore as a boil, it's according to Hoyle
    To cock your revolver and die.
But the code of a man who says fight all you can,
    And self-dissolution is barred;
In hunger and woe, oh it's easy to blow—
    It's the hell served for breakfast that's hard.

You're sick of the game? Well now, that's a shame!
    You're young and you're brave and you're bright.
You've had a raw deal, I know, but don't squeal.
    Buck up, do your damnedest and fight!
It's the plugging away that will win you the day,
    So don't be a piker, old pard;
Just draw on your grit; it's so easy to quit—
    It's the keeping your chin up that's hard.

It's easy to cry that you're beaten and die,
    It's easy to crawfish and crawl,
But to fight and to fight when hope's out of sight,
    Why, that's the best game of them all.
And though you come out of each grueling bout,
    All broken and beaten and scarred—
Just have one more try. It's dead easy to die,
    It's the keeping on living that's hard.

Robert W. Service

FRIENDS OF MINE

We like to be hospitable. To what should we be more hospitable than a glad spirit or a kind impulse?

GOOD MORNING, Brother Sunshine,
    Good morning, Sister Song,
I beg your humble pardon
    If you've waited very long.
I thought I heard you rapping,
    To shut you out were sin,
My heart is standing open,
    Won't you
      walk
        right
          in?

Good morning, Brother Gladness,
    Good morning, Sister Smile,
They told me you were coming,
    So I waited on a while.
I'm lonesome here without you,
    A weary while it's been,
My heart is standing open,
    Won't you
      walk
        right
          in?

Good morning, Brother Kindness,
　　Good morning, Sister Cheer,
I heard you were out calling,
　　So I waited for you here.
Some way, I keep forgetting
　　I have to toil or spin
When you are my companions,
　　Won't you
　　　　walk
　　　　　　right
　　　　　　　　in?

James W. Foley

THE WOMAN WHO UNDERSTANDS

"Is this the little woman that made this great war?" was Lincoln's greeting to Harriet Beecher Stowe. Often a woman is responsible for events by whose crash and splendor she herself is obscured. Often too she shapes the career of husband or brother or son. A man succeeds and reaps the honors of public applause, when in truth a quiet little woman has made it all possible—has by her tact and encouragement held him to his best, has had faith in him when his own faith has languished, has cheered him with the unfailing assurance, "You can, you must, you will."

*S*OMEWHERE *she waits to make you win, your soul*
　　in her firm white hands—
Somewhere the gods have made for you the Woman Who
　　Understands!

As the tide went out she found him
　　Lashed to a spar of Despair,
The wreck of his Ship around him—
　　The wreck of his Dreams in the air;
Found him and loved him and gathered
　　The soul of him close to her heart—
The soul that had sailed an uncharted sea,
The soul that had sought to win and be free—
　　The soul of which she was part!

And there in the dusk she cried to the man,
"Win your battle—you can, you can!"

Broken by Fate, unrelenting,
    Scarred by the lashings of Chance;
Bitter his heart-unrepenting—
    Hardened by Circumstance;
Shadowed by Failure ever,
    Cursing he would have died,
But the touch of her hand, her strong warm hand,
And her love of his soul, took full command,
    Just at the turn of the tide!
        Standing beside him, filled with trust,
        "Win!" she whispered, "you must, you must!"

Helping and loving and guiding,
    Urging when that were best,
Holding her fears in hiding
    Deep in her quiet breast;
This is the woman who kept him
    True to his standards lost,
When, tossed in the storm and stress of strife,
He thought himself through with the game of life.
    And ready to pay the cost.
        Watching and guarding, whispering still,
        "Win you can—and you will, you will!"

This is the story of ages,
    This is the Woman's way;
Wiser than seers or sages,
    Lifting us day by day;
Facing all things with a courage
    Nothing can daunt or dim,
Treading Life's path, wherever it leads—
Lined with flowers or choked with weeds,
    But ever with him—with him!

Guidon—comrade—golden spur—
The men who win are helped by her!

Somewhere she waits, strong in belief, your soul in her
*   firm white hands;*
Thank well the gods, when she comes to you—the Woman
*   Who Understands!*

Everard Jack Appleton

WANTED—A MAN

Business and the world are exacting in their demands upon us. They make no concessions to half-heartedness, incompetence, or plodding mediocrity. But for the man who has proved his worth and do the exceptional things with originality and sound judgment, they are eagerly watchful and have rich rewards.

YOU say big corporations scheme
    To keep a fellow down;
They drive him, shame him, starve him too
If he so much as frown.
God knows I hold no brief for them;
Still, come with me today
And watch those fat directors meet,
For this is what they say.

"In all our force not one to take
The new work that we plan!
In all the thousand men we've hired
Where shall we find a man?"

The world is shabby in the way
It treats a fellow too;
It just endures him while he works,
And kicks him when he's through.
It's ruthless; let him make good,
Or else it grabs its broom

And grumbles: "What a clutter's here!
We can't have this. Make room!"

And out he goes. It says, "Can bread
Be made from moldy bran?
The men come swarming here in droves,
But where'll I find a man?"

Yes, life is hard. But all the same
It seeks the man who's best.
Its grudging makes the prizes big;
The obstacles a test.
Don't ask to find the pathway smooth,
To march to fife and drum;
The plum-tree will not come to you;
Jack Horner, hunt the plum.

The eyes of life are yearning, sad,
As humankind they scan.
She says, "Oh, there are men enough,
But where'll I find a man?"

St. Clair Adams

IF I SHOULD DIE

A man whose word is as good as his bond is a man the world admires. It is related of Fox that a tradesman whom he long had owed money found him one day counting gold and asked for payment. Fox replied: "No; I owe this money to Sheridan. It is a debt of honor. If an accident should happen to me, he has nothing to show." The tradesman tore his note to pieces: "I change my debt into a debt of honor." Fox thanked him and handed over the money, saying that Sheridan's debt was not of so long standing and that Sheridan must wait. But most of us know men who are less scrupulous than Fox.

I F I should die tonight
And you should come to my cold corpse and say,
Weeping and heartsick o'er my lifeless clay—

If I should die tonight,
And you should come in deepest grief and woe—
And say; "Here's that ten dollars that I owe,"
   I might arise in my large white cravat
   And say, "What's that?"

   If I should die tonight
And you should come to my cold corpse and kneel,
Clasping my bier to show the grief you feel,
   I say, if I should die tonight
And you should come to me, and there and then
   Just even hint 'bout payin' me that ten,
   I might arise the while,
   But I'd drop dead again.

Ben King

JUST BE GLAD

   Misfortunes overtake us, difficulties confront us; but these things must not
induce us to give up. A congressman who had promised to be present at a polit-
ical meeting telegraphed at the last moment: "Cannot come; washout on the
line." "No need to stay away," said the answering telegram; "buy another shirt."

O HEART of mine, we shouldn't
   Worry so!
What we've missed of calm we couldn't
   Have, you know!
What we've met of stormy pain,
And of sorrow's driving rain,
We can better meet again,
   If it blow!

We have erred in that dark hour
   We have known,
When our tears fell with the shower,
   All alone!—
Were not shine and shower blent

As the gracious Master meant?—
Let us temper our content
    With His own.

For, we know, not every morrow
    Can be sad;
So, forgetting all the sorrow
    We have had,
Let us fold away our fears,
And put by our foolish tears,
And through all the coming years
    Just be glad.

James Whitcomb Riley

OPPORTUNITY

"I lack only one of having a hundred," said a student after an examination; "I have the two naughts." And all he did lack was a one, *rightly placed*. The world is full of opportunities. Discernment to perceive, courage to undertake, patience to carry through will change the whole aspect of the universe for us and bring positive achievement out of meaningless negation.

WITH doubt and dismay you are smitten
    You think there's no chance for you, son?
Why, the best books haven't been written
    The best race hasn't been run,
The best score hasn't been made yet,
    The best song hasn't been sung,
The best tune hasn't been played yet,
    Cheer up, for the world is young!

No chance? Why the world is just eager
    For things that you ought to create
Its store of true wealth is still meager
    Its needs are incessant and great,
It yearns for more power and beauty
    More laughter and love and romance,
More loyalty, labor and duty,

No chance—why there's nothing but chance!

For the best verse hasn't been rhymed yet,
    The best house hasn't been planned,
The highest peak hasn't been climbed yet,
    The mightiest rivers aren't spanned,
Don't worry and fret, faint hearted,
    The chances have just begun,
For the Best jobs haven't been started,
    The Best work hasn't been done.

Berton Braley

SOLITUDE

Said an Irishman who had several times been kicked downstairs: "I begin to think they don't want me around here." So it is with our sorrows, our struggles. Life decrees that they belong to us individually. If we try to make others share them, we are shunned. But struggling and weary humanity is glad enough to share our joys.

L AUGH and the world laughs with you;
  Weep and you weep alone;
  For the sad old earth
  Must borrow its mirth,
It has trouble enough of its own.

Sing, and the hills will answer;
Sigh, it is lost on the air;
  The echoes bound
  To a joyful sound,
But shrink from voicing care.

Rejoice, and men will seek you;
Grieve, and they turn and go;
  They want full measure
  Of all your pleasure,
But they do not want your woe.

Be glad, and your friends are many;
Be sad, and you lose them all;
  There are none to decline
  Your nectared wine,
But alone you must drink life's gall.

Feast, and your halls are crowded;
Fast, and the world goes by;
  Succeed and give,
  And it helps you live,
But it cannot help you die.

There is room in the halls of pleasure
For a long and lordly train;
  But one by one
  We must file on
Through the narrow aisles of pain.

Ella Wheeler Wilcox

UNSUBDUED

"An artist's career," said Whistler, "always begins tomorrow." So does the career of any man of courage and imagination. The Eden of such a man does not lie in yesterday. If he has done well, he forgets his achievements and dreams of the big deeds ahead. If he has been thwarted, he forgets his failures and looks forward to vast, sure successes. If fate itself opposes him, he defies it. Farragut's fleet was forcing an entrance into Mobile Bay. One of the vessels struck something, a terrific explosion followed, the vessel went down. "Torpedoes, sir." They scanned the face of the commander-in-chief. But Farragut did not hesitate. "Damn the torpedoes," said he. "Go ahead."

I HAVE hoped, I have planned, I have striven,
  To the Will I have added the deed;
The best that was in me I've given,
  I have prayed, but the gods would not heed.

I have dared and reached only disaster,
  I have battled and broken my lance;

I am bruised by a pitiless master
   That the weak and the timid call Chance.

I am old, I am bent, I am cheated
   Of all that Youth urged me to win;
But name me not with the defeated,
   Tomorrow again, I begin.

S.E. Kiser

HOW DID YOU DIE?

Grant at Ft. Donelson demanded unconditional and immediate surrender. At Appomattox he offered as lenient terms as victor ever extended to vanquished. Why the difference? The one event was at the beginning of the war, when the enemy's morale must be shaken. The other was at the end of the conflict, when a brave and noble adversary had been rendered helpless. In his quiet way Grant showed himself one of nature's gentlemen. He also taught a great lesson. No honor can be too great for the man, be he even our foe, who has steadily and uncomplainingly done his very best—and has failed.

DID you tackle that trouble that came your way
   With a resolute heart and cheerful?
Or hide your face from the light of day
   With a craven soul and fearful?
Oh, a trouble's a ton, or a trouble's an ounce,
   Or a trouble is what you make it,
And it isn't the fact that you're hurt that counts,
   But only how did you take it?

You are beat to earth? Well, well, what's that!
   Come up with a smiling face.
It's nothing against you to fall down flat,
   But to lie there—that's disgrace.
The harder you're thrown, why the higher you bounce;
   Be proud of your blackened eye!
It isn't the fact that you're licked that counts;
   It's how did you fight—and why?

And though you be done to the death, what then?
    If you battle the best you could,
If you played your part in the world of men,
    Why, the Critic will call it good.
Death comes with a crawl, or comes with a pounce,
    And whether he's slow or spry,
It isn't the fact that you're dead that counts,
    But only how did you die?

Edmund Vance Cooke

A LESSON FROM HISTORY

To break the ice of an undertaking is difficult. To cross on broken ice, as
Eliza did to freedom, or to row amid floating ice, as Washington did to victory,
is harder still. This poem applies especially to those who are discouraged in a
struggle to which they are already committed.

EVERYTHING'S easy after it's done;
    Every battle's a "cinch" that's won;
Every problem is clear that's solved—
The earth was round when it *revolved!*
But Washington stood amid grave doubt
With enemy forces camped about;
He could not know how he would fare
Till *after* he'd crossed the Delaware.

Thought the river was full of ice
He did not think about it twice,
But started across in the dead of night,
The enemy waiting to open the fight.
Likely feeling pretty blue,
Being human, same as you,
But he was brave amid despair,
And Washington crossed the Delaware!

So when you're with trouble beset,
And your spirits are soaking wet,

When all the sky with clouds is black,
Don't lie down upon your back
And look at *them*. Just do the thing;
Though you are choked, still try to sing.
If times are dark, believe them fair,
And you will cross the Delaware!

Joseph Morris

RABBI BEN EZRA

(SELECTED VERSES)

To some people success is everything, and the easier it is gained the better.
To Browning success is nothing unless it is won by painful effort.   What
Browning values is struggle.   Throes, rebuffs, even failure to achieve what we
wish, are to be welcomed, for the effects of vigorous endeavor inweave them-
selves into our characters; moreover through struggle we lift ourselves from the
degradation into which the indolent fall.   In what we have gone through, see
where we erred and where we did wisely, watch the workings of universal laws,
and resolve to apply hereafter what we have hitherto learned.

THEN, welcome each rebuff
    That turns earth's smoothness rough,
Each sting that bids nor sit nor stand but go!
Be our joys three-parts pain!
Strive, and hold cheap the strain;
Learn, nor account the pang; dare, never grudge
    the throe!

For thence—a paradox
Which comforts while it mocks—
Shall life succeed in that it seems to fail:
What I aspired to be,
And was not, comforts me:
A brute I might have been, but would not sink
    i' the scale.

So, still within this life,
Though lifted o'er its strife,
Let me discern, compare, pronounce at last,
"This rage was right i' the main,
That acquiescence vain:

20

The Future I may face now I have proved the
  Past."

For more is not reserved
to man, with soul just nerved
To act tomorrow what he learns today:
Here, work enough to watch
The Master work, and catch
Hints of the proper craft, tricks of the tool's
  true play.

Robert Browning

TO MELANCHOLY

The last invitation anybody would accept is "Come, let us weep together."
If we keep melancholy at our house, we should be careful to have it under lock
and key, so that no one will observe it.

MELANCHOLY,
  Melancholy,
I've no use for you, by Golly!
Yet I'm going to keep you hidden
In some chamber dark, forbidden,
Just as though you were a prize, sir,
Made of gold, and I a miser—
Not because I think you joy,
          Melancholy!
Not for that I mean to hoard you,
Keep you close and lodge and board you
As I would my sisters, brothers,
Cousins, aunts, and old grandmothers,
But that you shan't bother others
With your sniffling, snuffling folly,
          Howling,
          Yowling,
  Melancholy.

John Kendrick Bangs

THE LION PATH

Admiral Dupont was explaining to Farragut his reasons for not taking his ironclads into Charleston harbor. "You haven't given me the main reason yet," said Farragut. "What's that?" "You didn't think you could do it." So the man who thinks he can't pass a lion, can't. But the man who thinks he can, can. Indeed, he oftentimes finds that the lion isn't really there at all.

I DARE not!—
　　　　　Look! the road is very dark—
The trees stir softly and the bushes shake,
The long grass rustles, and the darkness moves
Here! there! beyond—!
There's something crept across the road just now!
And you would have me go—?
Go *there*, through that live darkness, hideous
With stir of crouching forms that wait to kill?
Ah, *look*! See there! and there! and there again!
Great yellow, glassy eyes, close to the ground!
Look! Now the clouds are lighter I can see
The long slow lashing of the sinewy tails,
And the set quiver of strong jaws that wait—!
Go there? Not I! Who dares to go who sees
So perfectly the lions in the path?

Comes one who dares.
　　　　　　　Afraid at first, yet bound
On such high errand as no fear could stay.
Forth goes he, with lions in his path.
And then——?
　　　　　　　He dared a death of agony—
Outnumbered battle with the king of beasts—
Long struggles in the horror of the night—
Dared, and went forth to meet—O ye who fear!
Finding an empty road, with homely fields,

And fences, and the dusty roadside trees—
Some spitting kittens, maybe, in the grass.

Charlotte Perkins Gilman

THE ANSWER

Bob Fitzsimmons lacked the physical bulk of the men he fought, was ungainly in build and movement, and not infrequently got himself floored in the early rounds of his contests. But many people considered him the best fighter of his time for his weight. Not a favorite at first, he won the popular heart by making good. Of course he had great natural powers; from any position when the chance at last came he could dart forth a sudden, wicked blow that no human being could withstand. But more formidable still was the spirit which gave him cool and complete command of all his resources and made him most dangerous when he was on the verge of being knocked out.

WHEN the battle breaks against you and the crowd forgets to cheer
When the Anvil Chorus echoes with the essence of a jeer;
When the knockers start their panning in the knocker's
    nimble way
With a rap for all your errors and a josh upon your play—
There is one quick answer ready that will nail them on the
    wing
There is one replay forthcoming that will wipe away the
    sting;
There is one elastic comeback that will hold them, as it
    should—
Make good.

No matter where you finish in the mix-up or the row,
There are those among the rabble who will pan you
    anyhow;
But the entry who is sticking and delivering the stuff
Can listen to the yapping as he giggles up his cuff;
The loafer has no comeback and the quitter no reply
When the Anvil Chorus echoes, as it will, against the sky;

But there's one quick answer ready that will wrap them
  in a hood—
Make good.

Grantland Rice

THE WORLD IS AGAINST ME

Babe Ruth didn't complain that opposing pitchers tried to strike him out; he swung at the ball till he swatted it for four bases. Ty Cob didn't complain that whole teams worked wits and muscles overtime to keep him from stealing home; he pitted himself against them all and went galloping or hurdling or sliding in. What other men can do any man can do if he works long enough with a brave enough heart.

"THE world is against me," he said with a sigh.
  "Somebody stops every scheme that I try.
The world has me down and it's keeping me there;
I don't get a chance. Oh, the world is unfair!
When a fellow is poor then he can't get a show;
The world is determined to keep him down low."

"What of Abe Lincoln?" I asked. "Would you say
That he was much richer than you are today?
He hadn't your chance of making his mark,
And his outlook was often exceedingly dark;
Yet he clung to his purpose with courage most grim
And he got to the top. Was the world against him?

"What of Ben Franklin? I've oft heard it said
That many a time he went hungry to bed.
He started with nothing but courage to climb,
But patiently struggled and waited his time.
He dangled awhile from real poverty's limb,
Yet he got to the top. Was the world against him?

"I could name you a dozen, yes, hundreds, I guess,
Of poor boys who've patiently climbed to success;
All boys who were down and who struggled alone,

Who'd have thought themselves rich if your fortune
    they'd known.
Yet they rose in the world you're so quick to condemn,
And I'm asking you now, was the world against them?"

Edgar A. Guest

SAY NOT THE STRUGGLE NOUGHT AVAILETH

In any large or prolonged enterprise we are likely to take too limited a view
of the progress we are making. The obstacles do not yield at some given point;
we therefore imagine we have made no headway. The poet here uses three com-
parisons to show the folly of accepting this hasty and partial evidence. A soldier
may think, from the little part of the battle he can see, that the day is going
against him; but by holding his ground stoutly he may help his comrades in
another quarter to win the victory. Successive waves may seem to rise no high-
er on the land, but far back in swollen creek and inlet is proof that the tide is
coming in. As we look toward the east, we are discouraged at the slowness of
daybreak; but by looking westward we see the whole landscape illumined.

S AY not the struggle nought availeth,
    The labor and the wounds are vain,
The enemy faints not, nor faileth,
    And as things have been they remain.

If hopes were dupes, fears may be liars;
    It may be, in yon smoke conceal'd,
Your comrades chase e'en now the fliers,
    And, but for you, possess the field.

For while the tired waves, vainly breaking,
    Seem here no painful inch to gain,
Far back, through creeks and inlets making,
    Comes silent, flooding in, the main.

And not by eastern windows only,
    When daylight comes, comes in the light,
In front, the sun climbs slow, how slowly,
    But westward, look, the land is bright.

Arthur Hugh Clough

WORTH WHILE

A little boy whom his mother had rebuked for not turning a deaf ear to temptation protested, with tears, that he had no deaf ear. But temptation, even when heard, must somehow be resisted. Yea, especially when heard! We deserve no credit for resisting it unless it comes to our ears like the voice of the siren.

IT is easy enough to be pleasant,
　　When life flows by like a song,
But the man worthwhile is one who will smile,
　　When everything goes dead wrong.
For the test of the heart is trouble,
　　And it always comes with the years,
And the smile that is worth the praises of earth,
　　Is the smile that shines through the tears.

It is easy enough to be prudent,
　　When nothing tempts you to stray,
When without or within no voice of sin
　　Is luring your soul away;
But it's only a negative virtue
　　Until it is tried by fire,
And the life that is worth the honor on earth,
　　Is the one that resists desire.

By the cynic, the sad, the fallen,
　　Who had no strength for the strife,
The world's highway is cumbered today,
　　They make up the sum of life.
But the virtue that conquers passion,
　　And the sorrow that hides in a smile,
It is these that are worth the homage on earth
　　For we find them but once in a while.

Ella Wheeler Wilcox

HOPE

Gloom and despair are really ignorance in another form. They fail to reckon with the fact that what appears to be baneful often turns out to be good. Lincoln lost the senatorship to Douglas and thought he had ended his career; had he won the contest, he might have remained only a senator. Life often has surprise parties for us. Things come to us masked in gloom and black; but Time, the revealer, strips off the disguise, and lo, what we have is blessings.

NEVER go gloomy, man with a mind,
    Hope is a better companion than fear;
Providence, ever benignant and kind,
    Gives with a smile what you take with a tear;
        All will be right,
        Look to the light.
Morning was ever the daughter of night;
All that was black will be all that is bright,
    Cheerily, cheerily, then cheer up.

Many a foe is a friend in disguise,
    Many a trouble a blessing most true,
Helping the heart to be happy and wise,
    With lover ever precious and joys ever new.
        Stand in the van,
        Strike like a man!
This is the bravest and cleverest plan;
Trusting in God while you do what you can.
    Cheerily, cheerily, then cheer up.

Anonymous

I'M GLAD

I'M glad the sky is painted blue;
    And the earth is painted green;
And such a lot of nice fresh air
    All sandwiched in between.

Anonymous

THE CHAMBERED NAUTILUS

The nautilus is a small mollusk that creeps upon the bottom of the sea, though it used to be supposed to swim, or even to spread a kind of sail so that the wind might drive it along the surface. What interests us in this poem is the way the nautilus grows. Just as a tree when sawed down has the record of its age in the number of rings, so does the nautilus measure its age by the ever-widening compartments of its shell. These it has successively occupied. The poet, looking upon the now empty shell, thinks of human life as growing in the same way. We advance from one state of being to another, each nobler than the one which preceded it, until the spirit leaves its shell altogether and attains a glorious and perfect freedom.

THIS is the ship of pearl, which, poets feign,
    Sailed the unshadowed main—
  The venturous bark that flings
On the sweet summer wind its purpled wings
In gulfs enchanted, where the Siren sings,
    And coral reefs lie bare,
Where the cold sea-maids rise to sun their streaming hair.

Its webs of living gauze no more unfurl;
    Wrecked is the ship of pearl!
    And every chambered cell,
Where its dim dreaming life was wont to dwell,
As the frail tenant shaped his growing shell,
    Before thee lies revealed—
Its irised ceiling rent, its sunless crypt unsealed!

Year after year beheld the silent toil
    That spread his lustrous coil;
    Still, as the spiral grew,
He left the past year's dwelling for the new,
Stole with soft step its shining archway through,
    Built up its idle door,
Stretched in his last-found home, and knew the old no
      more.

Thanks for the heavenly message brought by thee,
    Child of the wandering sea,
    Cast from her lap, forlorn!
From thy dead lips a clearer note is born
Than ever Triton blew from wreathéd horn!
    While on mine ear it rings,
Through the deep caves of thought I hear a voice that sings:

Build thee more stately mansions, O my soul,
    As the swift seasons roll!
    Leave thy low-vaulted past!
Let each new temple, nobler than the last,
Shut thee from heaven with a dome more vast,
    Till thou at length art free,
Leaving thine outgrown shell by life's unresting sea!

Oliver Wendell Holmes

PIPPA'S SONG

This little song vibrates with an optimism that embraces the whole universe. A frequent error in quoting it is the substitution of the word well for right. Browning is no such shallow optimist as to believe that all is well with the world, but he does maintain that things are right with the world, for in spite of its present evils it is slowly working its way toward perfection, and in the great scheme of things it may make these evils themselves an instrument to move it toward its ultimate goal.

THE year's at the spring
And day's at the morn;
Morning's at seven;
The hillside's dew-pearled;
The lark's on the wing;
The snail's on the thorn;
God's in his heaven—
All's right with the world.

Robert Browning

OWNERSHIP

The true value of anything lies not in the object itself or in its legal possession but in our attitude to it. We may own a thing in fee simple yet derive from it nothing but vexation. For those who have little, as indeed for those who have much, there are no surer means of happiness than enjoying that which they do not possess. Emerson shows us that two harvests may be gathered from every field—a material one by the man who raised the crop and an esthetic or spiritual one by whosoever can see beauty or thrill with an inner satisfaction.

THEY ride in Lincolns, those swell guys,
  While I can't half afford a Ford;
Choice fillets fill a void for them,
We've cheese and prunes the place I board;
They've smirking servants hanging round,
You'd guess by whom my shoes are shined.
But all the same I'm rich as they,
For ownership's a state of mind.

  They own, you say? Pshaw, they possess!
And what a fellow has, has him!
The rich can't stop and just enjoy
Their lawns and shrubs and house-fronts trim.
They're tied indoors and foot the bills;
I stroll or stray, as I'm inclined—
Possession was not meant for use,
But ownership's a state of mind.

  The folks who have must try to keep
Against the thieves who swarm and steal;
They dare not stride, they mince along—
Their pavement's a banana peel.
Who owns, the jeweler or I,
Yon gems by window-bars confined?
Possession lies in locks and keys;
True ownership's a state of mind.

I own my office (I've a boss,
But so have all men—so has he);
The business is not mine, but yet
I own the whole blamed company;
Stockholders are less proud than I
When competition's auld lang syned.
What care I that the profit's theirs?
I have what counts—an owner's mind.

The pretty girls I meet are mine
(I do not choose to tell them so);
I own the flowers, the trees, the birds;
I own the sunshine and the snow;
I own the block, I own the town—
The smiles, the songs of humankind.
For ownership is how you feel;
It's just a healthy state of mind.

St. Clair Adams

A SMILING PARADOX

Good nature or ill is like the loaves and fishes. The more we give away, the more we have.

I'VE squandered smiles today,
 And, strange to say,
Altho' my frowns with care I've stowed away,
Tonight I'm poorer far in frowns than at the start;
 While in my heart,
Wherein my treasures best I store,
I find my smiles increased by several score.

John Kendrick Bangs

THE NEW DUCKLING

There are people who, without having anything exceptional in their natures or purposes or visions, yet try to be different for the sake of being different. They are not content to be what they are; they wish to be "utterly other." Of course, they are hollow, artificial, insincere; moreover, they are nuisances. Their very foundations are wrong ones. Be yourself unless you're a fool; in that case, of course, try to be somebody else.

"I WANT to be new," said the duckling.
   "O ho!" said the wise old owl,
While the guinea-hen cluttered off chuckling
   To tell all the rest of the fowl.

"I should like a more elegant figure,"
   That child of a duck went on.
"I should like to grow bigger and bigger,
   Until I could swallow a swan.

"I *won't* be the bond slave of habit,
   I *won't* have these webs on my toes.
I want to run round like a rabbit,
   A rabbit as red as a rose.

"I *don't* want to waddle like mother,
   Or quack like my silly old dad.
I want to be utterly other,
   And *frightfully* modern and mad."

"Do you know," said the turkey, "you're quacking!
   There's a fox creeping up throe' the rye;
And, if you're not utterly lacking,
   You'll make for the duck pond. Goodby!"

But the duckling was perky as perky.
   "Take care of your stuffing!" he called.
(This was horribly rude to a turkey!)
   "But you aren't a real turkey," he bawled.

"You're an Early-Victorian Sparrow!
   A fox is more fun than a sheep!

I shall show that *my* mind is not narrow
    And give him my feathers—to keep."

Now the curious end of this fable,
    So far as the rest ascertained,
Though they searched from the barn to the stable,
    Was that *only his feathers remained.*

So he *wasn't* the bond slave of habit,
    And he *didn't* have webs on his toes;
And *perhaps* he runs round like a rabbit,
    A rabbit as red as a rose.

                                    Alfred Noyes

CAN YOU SING A SONG?

Nothing lifts the spirit more than a song, especially the inward song of a worker who can sound it alike at the beginning of his task, in the heat of mid-day, and in the weariness and cool of the evening.

CAN you sing a song to greet the sun,
    Can you cheerily tackle the work to be done,
Can you vision it finished when only begun,
        Can you sing a song?

Can you sing a song when the day's half through,
When even the thought of the rest wearies you,
With so little done and so much to do,
        Can you sing a song?

Can you sing a song at the close of the day,
When weary and tired, the work's put away,
With the joy that it's done the best of the pay,
        Can you sing a song?

                                    Joseph Morris

KNOW THYSELF

It seems impossible that human beings could endure so much until we realize that they have endured it. The spirit of man performs miracles; it transcends the limitations of flesh and blood. It is like Uncle Remus's account of Brer Rabbit climbing a tree. "A rabbit couldn't do that," the little boy protested. "He did," Uncle Remus responded; "he was jes' 'bleeged to."

REINED by an unseen tyrant's hand,
Spurred by an unseen tyrant's will,
Aquiver at the fierce command
That goads you up the danger hill,
You cry: "O Fate, O Life, be kind!
Grant but an hour of respite—give
One moment to my suffering mind!
I can not keep the pace and live."
But Fate drives on and will not heed
The lips that beg, the feet that bleed.
Drives, while you faint upon the road,
Drives, with a menace for a goad;
With fiery reins of circumstance
Urging his terrible advance
The while you cry in your despair,
"The pain is more than I can bear!"

Fear not the goad, fear not the pace,
Plead not to fall from out the race—
It is your own Self driving you,
Your Self that you have never known,
Seeing your little self alone.
Your Self, high-seated charioteer,
Master of cowardice and fear,
Your Self that sees the shining length
Of all the fearful road ahead,
Knows that the terrors that you dread
Are pigmies to your splendid strength;
Strength you have never even guessed,
Strength that has never needed rest.

Your Self that holds the mastering rein,
Seeing beyond the sweat and pain
And anguish of your driven soul,
The patient beauty of the goal!

Fighting upon the terror field
Where man and Fate came breast to breast,
Pressed by a thousand foes to yield,
Tortured and wounded without rest,
You cried: "Be merciful, O Life—
The strongest spirit soon must break
Before this all-unequal strife,
This endless fight for failure's sake!"
But Fate, unheeding, lifting high
His sword, and thrust you through to die,
And then there came one strong and great,
Who towered high o'er Chance and Fate,
Who bound your wound and eased your pain
And bade you rise and fight again.
And from some source you did not guess
Gushed a great tide of happiness—
A courage mightier than the sun—
You rose and fought and, fighting, won!

It was your own Self saving you,
Your Self no man has ever known,
Looking on flesh and blood alone.
That Self that lives so close to God
As roots that feed upon the sod.
That one who stands behind the screen,
Looks through the window of your eyes—
A being out of Paradise.
The Self no human eye has seen,
The living one who never tires,
Fed by the deep eternal fires.
Your flaming Self, with two-edged sword,
Made in the likeness of the Lord,

Angel and guardian at the gate,
Master of Death and King of Fate!

Angela Morgan

JUST WHISTLE

There is a psychological benefit in the mere physical act of whistling. When
the body makes music, the spirit falls into harmonies too, and the discords that
assail us cease to make themselves heard.

WHEN times are bad an' folks are sad
    An' gloomy day by day,
Jest try your best at lookin' glad
    An' whistle 'em away.

Don't mind how troubles bristle,
Jest take a rose or thistle.
      Hold your own
An' change your tone
An' whistle, whistle, whistle!

A song is worth a world o' sighs.
    When red the lightnings play,
Look for the rainbow in the skies
    An' whistle 'em away.

Don't mind how troubles bristle,
The rose comes with the thistle.
      Hold your own
An' change your tone
An' whistle, whistle, whistle!

Each day comes with a life that's new,
    A strange, continued story
But still beneath a bend o' blue
    The world rolls on to glory.

Don't mind how troubles bristle,
Jest take a rose or thistle.,
   Hold your own
An' change your tone
An' whistle, whistle, whistle!

Frank L. Stanton

"MIGHT HAVE BEEN"

"Yes, it's pretty hard," the optimistic old woman admitted. "I have to get along with only two teeth, one in the upper jaw and one in the lower—but thank God, they meet."

HERE'S to "The days that might have been";
  Here's to "The life I might have led";
The fame I might have gathered in—
  The glory ways I might have sped.
Great "Might Have Been," I drink to you
  Upon a throne where thousands hail—
And then—there looms another view—
  I also "might have been" in jail.

O "Land of Might Have been," we turn
  With aching hearts to where you wait;
Where crimson fires of glory burn,
  And laurel crowns the guarding gate;
We may not see across your fields
  The sightless skulls that knew their woe—
The broken spears—the shattered shields—
  That "might have been" as truly so.

"Of all sad words of tongue or pen"—
  So wails the poet in his pain—
The saddest are, "It might have been,"
  And worldwide runs the dull refrain.
The saddest? Yes—but in the jar

This thought brings to me with its curse,
I sometimes think the gladdest are
"It might have been a blamed sight worse."

Grantland Rice

THE ONE

In our youth we picture ourselves as we will be in the future—not mere types of this or that kind of success, but above all and in all, Ideal Men. Then come the years and the struggles, and we are buffeted and baffled, and our very ideal is eclipsed. But others have done better than we. Weary and harassed, they yet embody our visions. And we, if we are worth our salt, do not envy them when we see them. Nor should we grow dispirited. Rather should we rejoice in their triumph, rejoice that our dreams were not impossibilities, take courage to strive afresh for that which we know is best.

I KNEW his face the moment that he passed
    Triumphant in the thoughtless, cruel throng—
Triumphant, though the quiet, tired eyes
    Showed that his soul had suffered overlong.
And though across his brow faint lines of care
Were etched, somewhat of Youth still lingered there.
I gently touched his arm—he smiled at me—
He was the Man that Once I Meant to Be!

Where I had failed, he'd won from life, Success;
    Where I had stumbled, with sure feet he stood;
Alike—yet unalike—we faced the world,
    And through the stress he found that life was good.
And I? The bitter wormwood in the glass,
The shadowed way along which failures pass!
Yet as I saw him thus, joy came to me—
He was the Man that Once I Meant to Be!

I knew him! And I knew he knew me for
    The man HE might have been. Then did his soul
Thank silently the gods that gave him strength

To win, while I so sorely missed the goal?
He turned, and quickly in his own firm hand
He took my own—the gulf of Failure spanned,...
And that was all—strong, self-reliant, free,
He was the Man that Once I Meant to Be!

We did not speak. But in his sapient eyes
    I saw the spirit that had urged him on,
The courage that had held him through the fight
    Had once been mine, I thought, "Can it be gone?"
He felt that unasked question—felt it so
His pale lips formed the one-word answer, "No!"

    •   •   •   •   •

Too late to win? No! Not too late for me—
He is the Man that Still I Mean to Be!

Everard Jack Appleton

THE JOY OF LIVING

    Men too often act as if life were nothing more than hardships to be endured and difficulties to be overcome. They look upon what is happy or inspiring with eyes that really fail to see. As Wordsworth says of Peter Bell,

> "A primrose by the river's brim
> A yellow primrose was to him,
> And it was nothing more."

But to stop now and then and realize that the world is fresh and buoyant and happy, will do much to keep the spirit young. We should be glad that we are alive, should tell ourselves often in the words of Charles Lamb: "I am in love with this green earth."

THE south wind is driving
  His splendid cloud-horses
Through vast fields of blue.
The bare woods are singing,
The brooks in their courses
Are bubbling and springing
And dancing and leaping,

The violets peeping.
I'm glad to be living:
Aren't you?

Gamaliel Bradford

THERE WILL ALWAYS BE SOMETHING TO DO

An old lady, famous for her ability to find in other people traits that she could commend, was challenged to say a good word for the devil. After a moment's hesitation she answered, "You must at least give him credit for being industrious." Perhaps it is this superactivity of Satan that causes beings less wickedly inclined to have such scope for the exercise of their qualities. Certain it is that nobody need hang back from want of something to do, to promote, to assail, to protect, to endure, or to sympathize with.

THERE will always be something to do, my boy;
   There will always be wrongs to right;
There will always be need for a manly breed
   And men unafraid to fight.
There will always be honor to guard, my boy;
   There will always be hills to climb,
And tasks to do, and battles new
   From now till the end of time.

There will always be dangers to face, my boy;
   There will always be goals to take;
Men shall be tried, when the roads divide,
   And proved by the choice they make.
There will always be burdens to bear, my boy;
   There will always be need to pray;
There will always be tears through the future years,
   As loved ones are borne away.

There will always be God to serve, my boy,
   And always the Flag above;
They shall call to you until life is through
   For courage and strength and love.

So these are things that I dream, my boy,
  And have dreamed since your life began:
That whatever befalls, when the old world calls,
  It shall find you a sturdy man.

Edgar A. Guest

GOOD INTENTIONS

Thinking you would like a square meal will not in itself earn you one. Thinking you would like a strong body will not without effort on your part make you an athlete. Thinking you would like to be kind or successful will not bring you gentleness or achievement if you stop with mere thinking. The arrows of intention must have the bow of strong purpose to impel them.

THE road to hell, they assure me,
  With good intentions is paved;
And I know my desires are noble,
But my deeds might brand me depraved.
It's the warped grain in our nature,
And St. Paul has written it true:
"The good that I would I do not;
But the evil I would not I do."

I've met few men who are monsters
When I came to know them inside;
Yet their bearing and dealings external
Are crusted with cruelty, pride,
Scorn, selfishness, envy, indifference,
Greed—why the long list pursue?
The good that they would they do not;
But the evil they would not they do.

Intentions may still leave us beast-like;
With unchangeable purpose we're men.
We must drive the nail home—and then clinch it
Or storms shake it loose again.
In things of great import, in trifles,

We our recreant souls must subdue
Till the evil we would not we do not
And the good that we would we do.

St. Clair Adams

PHILOSOPHY FOR CROAKERS

Many people seem to get pleasure in seeing all the bad there is and in making everything about them gloomy. They are like the old woman who, on being asked how her health was, replied: "Thank the Lord, I'm poorly."

SOME folks git a heap o' pleasure
Out o' lookin' glum;
Hoard their cares like it was treasure—
Fear they won't have some.
Wear black border on their spirit;
Hang their hopes with crape;
Future's gloomy and they fear it,
Sure there's no escape.

Now there ain't no use of whinin'
Weightin' joy with lead;
There is silver in the linin'
Somewhere on ahead.

Can't enjoy the sun today—
It may rain tomorrow;
When a pain won't come their way,
Future pains they borrow.
If there's good news to be heard,
Ears are stuffed with cotton;
Evils dire are often inferred;
Good is all forgotten.

When upon a peel I stand,
Slippin' like a goner,

Luck, I trust, will shake my hand
    Just around the corner.

Keep a scarecrow in the yard,
    Fierce old bulldog near 'em;
Chase off joy that's tryin' hard
    To come in an' cheer 'em.
Wear their blinders big and strong,
    Dodge each happy sight;
Like to keep their faces long;
    Think the day is night.

        Now I've had my share of trouble
            Back been bent with ill;
        Big load makes the joy seem double
            When I mount the hill.

Got the toothache in their soul;
    Corns upon their feelin's;
Get their share but want the whole,
    Say it's crooked dealin's.
Natures steeped in indigo;
    Got their joy-wires crossed;
Swear it's only weeds that grow;
    Flowers always lost.

        Now it's best to sing a song
            'Stead o' sit and mourn;
        Rose you'll find grows right along
            Bigger than the thorn.

Beat the frogs the way they croak;
    See with goggles blue—
Universe is cracked or broke
    'Bout to split in two.
Think the world is full of sin,

Soon go up the spout;
Badness always movin' in,
Goodness movin' out.

But I've found folks good and kind,
'Cause I thought they would be;
Most men try, at least I find,
To be what they should be.

Joseph Morris

THE FIGHTING FAILURE

"I'm not a rabid, preachy, pollyanna optimist. Neither am I a gloomy grouch. I believe in a loving Divine Providence Who expects you to play the Game to the limit, Who wants you to hold tight to His hand, and Who compensates you for the material losses by giving you the ability to retain your sense of values and keep your spiritual sand out of the bearings of your physical machine, if you'll trust and —'Keep Sweet, Keep Cheerful, or else—Keep Still.'"—*Everard Jack Appleton*

HE has come the way of the fighting men, and fought
by the rules of the Game,
And out of Life he has gathered—What? A living—
and little fame,
Ever and ever the Goal looms near—seeming each time
worth while;
But ever it proves a mirage fair—ever the grim gods
smile.
And so, with lips hard set and white, he buries the hope
that is gone—
His fight is lost—and he knows it is lost—and yet he is
fighting on.

Out of the smoke of the battle-line watching men win
their way,
And, cheering with those who cheer success, he enters
again the fray,

Licking the blood and the dust from his lips, wiping the
sweat from his eyes,
He does the work he is set to do—and "therein honor
lies."
Brave they were, these men he cheered—theirs is the
winner's thrill;
His fight is lost—and he knows it is lost—and yet he is
fighting still.

And those who won have rest and peace; and those who
died have more;
But, weary and spent, he can not stop seeking the ultimate
score;
Courage was theirs for a little time—but what of the
man who sees
That he must lose, yet will not beg mercy upon his
knees?
Side by side with grim Defeat he struggles at dusk or
dawn—
His fight is lost—and he know it is lost—and yet he is
fighting on.

Praise for the warriors who succeed, and tears for the
vanquished dead;
The world will hold them close to her heart, wreathing
each honored head,
But there in the ranks, soul-sick, time-tired, he battles
against the odds,
Sans hope, but true to his colors torn, the plaything of
the gods!
Uncover when he goes by, at last! Held to his task by
will
The fight is lost—and he know it is lost—and yet he is
fighting still!

Everard Jack Appleton

DUTY

In a single sentence Emerson crystallizes the faith that nothing is impossible to those whose guide is duty. His words, though spoken primarily of youth, apply to the whole of human life.

S O nigh is grandeur to our dust,
So near is God to man,
When duty whispers low, Thou must,
The youth replies, I can.

Ralph Waldo Emerson

THE CALL OF THE UNBEATEN

P.T. Barnum had shrewdness, inventiveness, hair-trigger readiness in acting or deciding, an eye for hidden possibilities, an instinct for determining before-hand what would prove popular. All these qualities helped him in his original and extraordinary career. But the quality he valued most highly was the one he called "stick-to-it-iveness." This completed the others. Without it the great showman could not have succeeded at all. Nor did he think that any man who lacks it will make much headway in life.

W E know how rough the road will be,
How heavy here the load will be,
We know about the barricades that wait along the track;
But we have set our soul ahead
Upon a certain goal ahead
And nothing left from hell to sky shall ever turn us
back.

We know how brief all fame must be,
We know how crude the game must be,
We know how soon the cheering turns to jeering down
the block;
But there's a deeper feeling here
That Fate can't scatter reeling here,
In knowing we have battled with the final ounce in
stock.

We sing of no wild glory now,
Emblazoning some story now
    Of mighty charges down the field beyond some guarded
        pit;
But humbler tasks befalling us,
Set duties that are calling us,
    Where nothing left from hell to sky shall ever make
        us quit.

Grantland Rice

POLUNIUS'S ADVICE TO LAERTES

A father's advice to his son how to conduct himself in the world: Don't tell all you think, or put into action thoughts out of harmony or proportion with the occasion. Be friendly, but not common; don't dull your palm by effusively shaking hands with every chance newcomer. Avoid quarrels if you can, but if they are forced on you, give a good account of yourself. Hear every man's censure (opinion), but express your own ideas to few. Dress well but not ostentatiously. Neither borrow nor lend. And guarantee yourself against being false to others by setting up the high moral principle of being true to yourself.

G IVE thy thoughts no tongue,
    Nor any unproportion'd thought his act.
Be thou familiar but by no means vulgar;
The friends thou hast, and their adoption tried,
Grapple them to thy soul with hoops of steel;
But do not dull thy palm with entertainment
Of each new-hatch'd, unfledg'd comrade. Beware
Of entrance to a quarrel, but, being in,
Bear 't that th' opposed may beware of thee.
Give every man's censure, but reserve thy judgment.
Costly thy habit as thy purse can buy,
But not express'd in fancy; rich, not gaudy;
For the apparel oft proclaims the man.

   •   •   •   •   •

  Neither a borrower, nor a lender be;
For loan oft loses both itself and friend,
And borrowing dulls the edge of husbandry.

This above all: to thine own self be true,
And it must follow, as night the day,
Though canst not then be false to any man.

William Shakespeare

HOW DO YOU TACKLE YOUR WORK?

It would be foolish to begin digging a tunnel through a mountain with a mere pick and spade. We must assemble for the task great mechanical contrivances. And so with our energies of will; a slight tool means a slight achievement; a huge, aggressive engine, driving on at full blast, means corresponding bigness of results.

HOW do you tackle your work each day?
Are you scared of the job you find?
Do you grapple the task that comes your way
    With a confident, easy mind?
Do you stand right up to the work ahead
    Or fearfully pause to view it?
Do you start to toil with a sense of dread
    Or feel that you're going to do it?

You can do as much as you think you can,
    But you'll never accomplish more;
If you're afraid of yourself, young man,
    There's little for you in store.
For failure comes from the inside first,
    It's there if we only knew it,
And you can win, though you face the worst,
    If you feel that you're going to do it.

Success! It's found in the soul of you,
    And not in the realm of luck!
The world will furnish the work to do,
    But you must provide the pluck.
You can do whatever you think you can,
    It's all in the way you view it.
It's all in the start you make, young man:

You must feel that you're going to do it.

How do you tackle your work each day?
    With confidence clear, or dread?
What to yourself do you stop and say
    When a new task lies ahead?
What is the thought that is in your mind?
    Is fear ever running through it?
If so, just tackle the next you find
    By thinking you're going to do it.

Edgar A. Guest

MAN OR MANIKIN

The world does not always distinguish between appearance and true merit Pretence often gets the plaudits, but desert is above them—it has rewards of its own.

NO matter whence you came, from a palace or a ditch,
    You're a man, man, man, if you square yourself to life;
And no matter what they say, hermit-poor or Midas-rich,
You are nothing but a husk if you sidestep strife.

For it's do, do, do, with a purpose all your own,
That makes a man a man, whether born a serf or king;
And it's loaf, loaf, loaf, lolling on a bench or throne
That makes a being thewed to act a limp and useless thing!

No matter what you do, miracles or fruitless deeds,
You're a man, man, man, if you do them with a will;
And no matter how you loaf, cursing wealth or mumbling
    creeds,
You are nothing but a noise, and its weight is nil.

For it's be, be, be, champion of your heart and soul,
That makes a man a man, whether reared in silk or rags;

And it's talk, talk, talk, from a tattered shirt or store,
That makes the image of a god a manikin that brags.

Richard Butler Glaenzer

HAVING DONE AND DOING
(Adapted from "Troilus and Cressida")

A member of Parliament, having succeeded notably in his maiden effort at speech-making, remained silent through the rest of his career lest he should not duplicate his triumph. This course was stupid; in time the address which had brought him fame became a theme for disparagement and mockery. A man cannot rest on his laurels, else he will soon lack the laurels to rest on. If he has true ability, he must from time to time show it, instead of asking us to recall what he did in the past. There is a natural instinct which makes the whole world kin. It is distrust of a mere reputation. It is a hankering to be shown. Unless the evidence to set us right is forthcoming, we will praise dust which is gilded over rather than gold which is dusty from disuse.

TIME hath, my lord, a wallet at his back,
Wherein he puts alms for oblivion,
A great-sized monster of ingratitudes:
Those scraps are good deeds past: which are devoured
As fast as they are made, forgot as soon
As done: perseverance, dear my lord,
Keeps honor bright: to have done is to hang
Quite out of fashion like a rusty mail
In monumental mockery. Take the instant way;
For honor travels in a strait so narrow
Where one but goes abreast; keep, then, the path;
For emulation hath a thousand sons
That one by one pursue: if you give way
Or hedge aside from the direct forthright,
Like to an entered tide they all rush by
And leave you hindmost;
Or, like a gallant horse fallen in first rank,
Lie there for pavement to the abject rear,
O'errun and trampled on: then what they do in present,
Though less than yours in past, must o'ertop yours;

For time is like a fashionable host
That slightly shakes his parting guest by the hand,
And with his arms outstretched, as he would fly,
Grasps in the corner: welcome ever smiles,
And farewell goes out sighing. O! let not virtue seek
Remuneration for the thing it was; for beauty, wit,
High birth, vigor of bone, desert in service,
Love, friendship, charity, are subjects all
To envious and calumniating time.
One touch of nature makes the whole world kin,
That all with one consent praise new-born gawds,
Though they are made and molded of things past,
And give to dust that is a little gilt
More laud than gilt o'er-dusted.
The present eye praises the present object,
Since things in motion sooner catch the eye
Than what not stirs.

William Shakespeare

FAITH

Faith is not a passive thing—mere believing or waiting. It is an active thing—a positive striving and achievement, even if conditions be untoward.

FAITH is not merely praying
    Upon your knees at night;
Faith is not merely straying
    Through darkness to the light.

Faith is not merely waiting
    For glory that may be,
Faith is not merely hating
    The sinful ecstasy.

Faith is the brave endeavor
    The splendid enterprise,

The strength to serve, whatever
Conditions may arise.

S. E. Kiser

OPPORTUNITY

What is opportunity? To the brilliant mind of Senator Ingalls it is a stupendous piece of luck. It comes once and once only to every human being, wise or foolish, good or wicked. If it be not perceived on the instant, it passes by forever. No longing for it, no effort, can bring it back. Notice that this view is fatalistic; it makes opportunity an external thing—one that enriches men or leaves their lives empty without much regard to what they deserve.

MASTER of human destinies am I!
  Fame, love, and fortune on my footsteps wait.
Cities and fields I walk; I penetrate
Deserts and seas remote, and passing by
Hovel and mart and palace—soon or late
I knock, unbidden, once at every gate!
If sleeping, wake—if feasting, rise before
I turn away. It is the hour of fate,
And they who follow me reach every state
Mortals desire, and conquer every foe
Save death; but those who doubt or hesitate,
Condemned to failure, penury, and woe,
Seek me in vain and uselessly implore.
I answer not, and I return no more!

John James Ingalls

OPPORTUNITY

THERE is a tide in the affairs of men,
  Which, taken at the flood, leads on to fortune;
Omitted, all the voyage of their life
Is bound in shallows and in miseries.
On such a full sea are we now afloat;

And we must take the current when it serves,
Or lose our ventures.

William Shakespeare

OPPORTUNITY

To the thought of the preceding poem, we have here a direct answer. No matter how a man may have failed in the past, the door of opportunity is always open to him. He should not give way to useless regrets; he should know that the future is within his control, that it will be what he chooses to make it.

THEY do me wrong who say I come no more
    When once I knock and fail to find you in;
For every day I stand outside your door,
    And bid you wake, and rise to fight and win.

Wail not for precious chances passed away,
    Weep not for golden ages on the wane!
Each night I burn the records of the day—
    At sunrise every soul is born again!

Laugh like a boy at splendors that have sped,
    To vanished joys be blind and deaf and dumb;
My judgments seal the dead past with its dead,
    But never bind a moment yet to come.

Though deep in mire, wring not your hands and weep;
    I lend my arm to all who say "I can!"
No shame-faced outcast ever sank so deep,
    But yet might rise and be again a man!

Dost thou behold thy lost youth all aghast?
    Dost reel from righteous Retribution's blow?
Then turn from blotted archives of the past,
    And find the future's pages white as snow.

Art though a mourner? Rouse thee from thy spell;
　　Art thou a sinner? Sins may be forgiven;
Each morning gives thee wings to flee from hell,
　　Each night a star to guide thy feet to heaven.

Walter Malone

OPPORTUNITY

In this poem yet another view of opportunity is presented. The recreant or the dreamer complains that he has no real chance. He would succeed, he says, if he had but the implements of success—money, influence, social prestige, and the like. But success lies far less in implements than in the use we make of them. What one man throws away as useless, another man seizes as the best means of victory at hand. For every one of us the materials for achievement are sufficient. The spirit that prompts us is what ultimately counts.

THIS I beheld, or dreamed it in a dream—
　　There spread a cloud of dust along a plain;
And underneath the cloud, or in it, raged
A furious battle, and men yelled, and swords
Shocked upon swords and shields. A prince's
　　banner
Wavered, then staggered backward, hemmed by
　　foes.
A craven hung along the battle's edge,
And thought, "Had I a sword of keener steel—
That blue blade that the king's son bears—but
　　this
Blunt thing——!" he snapt and flung it from his
　　hand,
And lowering crept away and left the field.
Then came the king's son, wounded, sore bestead,
And weaponless, and saw the broken sword,
Hilt-buried in the dry and trodden sand,
And ran and snatched it, and with battle-shout
Lifted afresh he hewed his enemy down,
And saved a great cause that heroic day.

Edward Rowland Sill

MY PHILOSOPHY

Though dogs persist in barking at the moon, the moon's business is not to answer the dogs or to waste strength placating them but simply to shine. The man who strives or succeeds is sure to be criticized. Is he therefore to abstain from all effort? We are responsible for our own lives and cannot regulate them according to other people's ideas. "Whoso would be a man," says Emerson, "must be a nonconformist."

I ALLUS argy that a man
  Who does about the best he can
Is plenty good enough to suit
This lower mundane institute—
No matter ef his daily walk
Is subject fer his neghbor's talk,
And critic-minds of ev'ry whim
Jest all git up and go fer him!

    •   •   •   •   •

It's natchurl enough, I guess,
When some gits more and some gits less,
Fer them-uns on the slimmest side
To claim it ain't a fare divide;
And I've knowed some to lay and wait,
And git up soon, and set up late,
To ketch some feller they could hate
For goin' at a faster gait.

    •   •   •   •   •

My doctern is to lay aside
Contensions, and be satisfied:
Jest do your best, and praise er blame
That follers that, counts jest the same.
I've allus noticed grate success
Is mixed with troubles, more er less,
And it's the man who does the best
That gits more kicks than all the rest.

James Whitcomb Riley

ULYSSES

Ulysses is shot through and through with the spirit of strenuous and never-ceasing endeavor—a spirit manifest in a hero who has every temptation to rest and enjoy. Ulysses is old. After 10 long years of warfare before Troy, after endless misfortunes on his homeward voyage, after travels and experiences that have taken him everywhere and shown him everything that men know and do, he has returned to his rude native kingdom. He is reunited with his wife Penelope and his son Telemachus. He is rich and famous. Yet he is unsatisfied. The task and routine of governing a slow, materially mind people, though suited to his son's temperament, are unsuited to his. He wants to wear out rather than to rust out. He wants to discover what the world still holds. He wants to drink life to the lees. The morning has passed, the long day has waned, twilight and the darkness are at hand. But scant as are the years left to him, he will use them in a last, incomparable quest. He rallies his old comrades—tried men who always

> "With a frolic welcome took
> The thunder and the sunshine..."

and asks them to brave with him once more the hazards and the hardships of the life of vast, unsubdued enterprise.

IT little profits that an idle king,
By this still hearth, among these barren crags,
Match'd with an aged wife, I mete and dole
Unequal laws unto a savage race,
That hoard, and sleep, and feed, and know not me.
I cannot rest from travel; I will drink
Life to the lees. All times I have enjoy'd
Greatly, have suffer'd greatly, both with those
That love me, and alone; on shore, and when
Thro' scudding drifts the rainy Hyades
Vext the dim sea. I am become a name;
For always roaming with a hungry heart
Much have I seen and known—cities of men
And manners, climates, councils, governments,
Myself not least, but honor'd of them all—
And drunk delight of battle with my peers,
Far on the ringing plains of windy Troy.

I am a part of all that I have met;
Yet all experience is an arch wherethro'
Gleams that untravell'd world whose margin fades
For ever and for ever when I move.
How dull it is to pause, to make an end,
To rust unburnish'd, not to shine in use!
As tho' to breathe were life! Life piled on life
Were all too little, and of one to me
Little remains; but every hour is saved
From that eternal silence, something more,
A bringer of new things; and vile it were
For some three suns to store and hoard myself,
And this gray spirit yearning in desire
To follow knowledge like a sinking star,
Beyond the utmost bound of human thought.

     This is my son, mine own Telemachus,
To whom I leave the sceptre and isle—
Well-beloved of me, discerning to fulfill
This labor, by slow prudence to make mild
A rugged people, and thro' soft degrees
Subdue them to the useful and the good.
Most blameless is he, centered in the sphere
Of common duties, decent not to fail
In offices of tenderness, and pay
Meet adoration to my household gods,
When I am gone. He works his work, I mine.

     There lies the port; the vessel puffs her sail;
There gloom the dark, broad seas. My mariners,
Souls that have toil'd, and wrought, and thought
      with me—
That ever with a frolic welcome took
The thunder and the sunshine, and opposed
Free hearts, free foreheads—you and I are old;
Old age hath yet his honor and his toil.
Death closes all; but something ere the end,
Some work of noble note, may yet be done,

Not unbecoming men that strove with Gods.
The lights begin to twinkle from the rocks;
The long day wanes; the slow moon climbs; the deep
Moans round with many voices. Come, my friends.
'Tis not too late to seek a newer world.
Push off, and sitting well in order smite
The sounding furrows; for my purpose holds
To sail beyond the sunset, and the baths
Of all the western stars, until I die.
It may be that the gulfs will wash us down;
It may be we shall touch the Happy Isles,
And see the great Achilles, whom we knew.
Tho' much is taken, much abides; and tho'
We are not now that strength which in old days
Moved earth and heaven, that which we are, we are—
One equal temper of heroic hearts,
Made weak by time and fate, but strong in will
To strive, to seek, to find, and not to yield.

Alfred Tennyson

THE GIFTS OF GOD

What a wonderful feeling to complete a goal and sit back and bask in the pleasure of accomplishment, to say, "I did it." But this feeling doesn't last. After getting it done, another feeling emerges, one that nudges you and says, "Up and at 'em. Time for more." We are driven, but why? After reaching a certain point, why can't we say, "No need for more," then be content? We become discontented not for material gain but to progress spiritually. Ours is a divine discontent.

WHEN God at first made Man,
  Having a glass of blessings standing by;
Let us (said He) pour on him all we can:
Let the world's riches, which disperséd lie,
   Contract into a span.

  So Strength first made a way;
Then beauty flow'd, then wisdom, honor, pleasure:

When almost all was out, God made a stay,
Perceiving that alone, of all His treasure,
    Rest in the bottom lay.

For if I should (said He)
Bestow this jewel also on My creature,
He would adore My gifts instead of Me,
And rest in Nature, not the God of Nature.
    So both should losers be.

Yet let him keep the rest,
But keep them with repining restlessness:
Let him be rich and weary, that at least,
If goodness lead him not, yet weariness
    May toss him to My breast.

George Herbert

PREPAREDNESS

FOR all your days prepare,
    And meet them ever alike:
When you are the anvil, bear—
    When you are the hammer, strike.

Edwin Markham

THE WISDOM OF FOLLY

"Jog on, jog on, the footpath way,
And merrily hent the stile-a:
A merry heart goes all the day,
Your sad tires in a mile-a."

Shakespeare's lilting stanza conveys a great truth—the power of cheerfulness to give impetus and endurance. The *a* at the end of lines is merely an addition in singing; the word *hent* means take.

THE cynics say that every rose
   Is guarded by a thorn which grows
      To spoil our posies;
But I no pleasure therefore lack;
I keep my hands behind my back
      When smelling roses.

Though outwardly a gloomy shroud
The inner half of every cloud
      Is bright and shining:
I therefore turn my clouds about,
And always wear them inside out
      To show the lining.

My modus operandi this—
To take no heed of what's amiss;
      And not a bad one;
Because, as Shakespeare used to say,
A merry heart goes twice the way
      That tires a sad one.

Ellen Thorneycroft Fowler

SEE IT THROUGH

An American traveler in Italy stood watching a lumberman who, as the logs floated down a swift mountain stream, jabbed his hook in an occasional one and drew it carefully aside. "Why do you pick out those few?" the traveler asked. "They all look alike." "But they are not alike, seignior. The logs I let pass have grown on the side of a mountain, where they have been protected all their lives. Their grain is coarse; they are good only for lumber. But these logs, seignior, grew on the top of the mountain. From the time they were sprouts and saplings they were lashed and buffeted by the winds, and so they grew strong with fine grain. We save them for choice work; they are not 'lumber,' seignior."

WHEN you're up against a trouble,
   Meet it squarely, face to face;
Lift your chin and set your shoulders,
   Plant your feet and take a brace.

When it's vain to try to dodge it,
    Do the best that you can do;
You may fail, but you may conquer,
    See it through!

Black may be the clouds about you
    And your future may seem grim,
But don't let your nerve desert you;
    Keep yourself in fighting trim.
If the worse is bound to happen,
    Spite of all that you can do,
Running from it will not save you,
    See it through!

Even hope may seem but futile,
    When with troubles you're beset,
But remember you are facing
    Just what other men have met.
You may fail, but fall still fighting;
    Don't give up, whate'er you do;
Eyes front, head high to the finish.
    See it through!

Edgar A. Guest

DECEMBER 31

If January 1 is an ideal time for renewed consecration, December 31 is an ideal time for thankful reminiscence. The year has not brought us everything we might have hoped, but neither has it involved us in everything we might have feared. Many are the perils, the failures, the miseries we have escaped, and life to us is still gracious and wholesome and filled to the brim with satisfaction.

B EST day of all the year, since I
    May see thee pass and know
That if thou dost not leave me high
    Thou hast not found me low,
And since, as I behold thee die,

Thou leavest me the right to say
That I tomorrow still may vie
    With them that keep the upward way.

Best day of all the year to me,
    Since I may stand and gaze
Across the grayish past and see
    So many crooked ways
That might have led to misery,
    Or might have ended at Disgrace—
Best day since thou dost leave me free
    To look the future in the face.

Best day of all days of the year,
    That was so kind, so good,
Since thou dost leave me still the dear
    Old faith in brotherhood—
Best day since I, still striving here,
    May view the past with small regret,
And, undisturbed by doubts or fear,
    Seeks path that are untrod as yet.

S. E. Kiser

RING OUT, WILD BELLS

This great New Year's poem belongs almost as well to every day in the year, because it expresses a social ideal of justice and happiness.

R ING out, wild bells, to the wild sky,
    The flying cloud, the frosty light:
    The year is dying in the night;
Ring out, wild bells, and let him die.

Ring out the old, ring in the new,
    Ring, happy bells, across the snow:
    The year is going, let him go;
Ring out the false, ring in the true.

Ring out the grief that saps the mind,
    For those that here we see no more;
    Ring out the feud of rich and poor,
Ring in redress to all mankind.

Ring out a slowly dying cause,
    And ancient forms of party strife;
    Ring in the nobler modes of life,
With sweeter manners, purer laws.

Ring out the want, the care, the sin,
    The faithless coldness of the times;
    Ring out, ring out my mournful rhymes,
But ring the fuller minstrel in.

Ring out false pride in place and blood,
    The civic slander and the spite;
    Ring in the love of truth and right,
Ring in the common love of good.

Ring out old shapes of foul disease;
    Ring out the narrowing lust of gold;
    Ring out the thousand wars of old,
Ring in the thousand years of peace.

Ring in the valiant man and free,
    The larger heart, the kindlier hand;
    Ring out the darkness of the land,
Ring in the Christ that is to be.

Alfred Tennyson

WORK

The dog that dropped his bone to snap at its reflection in the water went dinnerless. So do we often lose the substance—the joy—of our work by longing for tasks we think better fitted to our capabilities.

L ET me but do my work from day to day,
In field or forest, at the desk or loom,
In roaring marketplace or tranquil room;
Let me but find it in my heart to say,
When vagrant wishes beckon me astray,
"This is my work; my blessing, not my doom:
Of all who live, I am the one by whom
This work can best be done in the right way."

Then shall I see it not too great, nor small,
To suit my spirit and to prove my powers;
Then shall I cheerful greet the laboring hours,
And cheerful turn, when the long shadows fall
At eventide, to play and love and rest,
Because I know for me my work is best.

Henry Van Dyke

START WHERE YOU STAND

When a man who had been in the penitentiary applied to Henry Ford for employment, he started to tell Mr. Ford his story. "Never mind," said Mr. Ford, "I don't care about the past. Start where you stand!"

S TART where you stand and never mind the past,
The past won't help you in beginning new,
If you have left it all behind at last
Why, that's enough, you're done with it, you're through;
This is another chapter in the book,
This is another race that you have planned,
Don't give the vanished days a backward look,
Start where you stand.

The world won't care about your old defeats
If you can start anew and win success,
The future is your time, and time is fleet
And there is much of work and strain and stress;
Forget the buried woes and dead despairs,

Here is a brand new trial right at hand,
The future is for him who does and dares,
   Start where you stand.

Old failures will not halt, old triumphs aid,
   Today's the thing, tomorrow soon will be;
Get in the fight and face it unafraid,
   And leave the past to ancient history;
What has been, has been; yesterday is dead
   And by it you are neither blessed nor banned,
Take courage, man, be brave and drive ahead,
   Start where you stand.

                                          Berton Braley

A HOPEFUL BROTHER

A Cripple Creek miner remarked that he had hunted for gold for 25 years.
He was asked how much he had found. "None," he replied, "but the prospects
are good."

EF you ask him, day or night,
   When the worl' warn't running right,
"Anything that's good in sight?"
This is allus what he'd say,
In his uncomplainin' way—
      Well, I'm hopin'."

When the winter days waz nigh,
An' the clouds froze in the sky,
Never sot him down to sigh.
But, still singin' on his way,
He'd stop long enough to say—
      "Well, I'm hopin'."

Dyin', asked of him that night
(Sperrit waitin' fer its flight),

"Brother, air yer prospec's bright?"
An'—last words they heard him say,
In the ol' sweet, cheerful way—
   "Well, I'm hopin'."

Frank L. Stanton

A SONG OF THANKSGIVING

We should have grateful spirits, not merely for personal benefits but also for the right to sympathize, to understand, to help, to trust, to struggle, to aspire.

THANK God I can rejoice
   In human things—the multitude's glad voice,
The street's warm surge beneath the city light,
The rush of hurrying faces on my sight,
The million-celled emotion in the press
That would their human fellowship confess.
Thank Thee because I may my brother feed,
That Thou has opened me unto his need,
Kept me from being callous, cold and blind,
Taught me the melody of being kind.
Thus, for my own and for my brother's sake—
   Thank Thee I am awake!

Thank Thee that I can trust!
That though a thousand times I feel the thrust
Of faith betrayed, I still have faith in man,
Believe him pure and good since time began—
Thy child forever, though he may forget
The perfect mold in which his soul was set.
Thank Thee that when love dies, fresh love springs up,
New wonders pour from Heaven's cup.
Young to my soul the ancient need returns,
Immortal in my heart the ardor burns;
My altar fires replenished from above—
   Thank Thee that I can love!

Thank Thee that I can hear,
Finely and keenly with the inner ear,
Below the rush and clamor of a throng
The mighty music of the under-song.
And when the day has journeyed to its rest,
Lo, as I listen, from the amber west,
Where the great organ lifts its glowing spires,
There sounds the chanting of the unseen choirs.
Thank Thee for sight that shows the hidden flame
Beneath all breathing, throbbing things the same,
Thy Pulse the pattern of the thing to be. . .
    Thank Thee that I can see!

Thank Thee that I can feel!
That though life's blade be terrible as steel,
My soul is stripped and naked to the fang,
I crave the stab of beauty and the pain.
To be alive,
To think, to yearn, to strive,
To suffer torture when the goal is wrong,
To be sent back and fashioned strong
Rejoicing in the lesson that was taught
By all the good the grim experience wrought;
At last, exulting, to *arrive.* . .
    Thank God I am alive!

Angela Morgan

LOSE THE DAY LOITERING

Anything is hard to begin, whether it be taking a cold shower, writing a letter, clearing up a misunderstanding, or getting on with the day's work. Yet "a thing begun is half done." No matter how unpleasant a thing is to do, begin it and immediately it becomes less unpleasant. Form the excellent habit of making a start.

LOSE the day loitering, 'twill be the same story
    Tomorrow, and the next more dilatory,
For indecision brings its own delays,
And days are lost lamenting o'er lost days.
Are you in earnest? Seize this very minute!
What you can do, or think you can, begin it!
Only engage, and then the mind grows heated;
Begin it, and the work will be completed.

                  Johann Wolfgang von Goethe

PLAYING THE GAME

We don't like the man who whines that the cards were stacked against him or that the umpire cheated. We admire the chap who, when he must take his medicine, takes it cheerfully, bravely. To play the game steadily is a merit, whether the game be a straight one or crooked. A thoroughbred, even though bad, has more of our respect than the craven who cleaves to the proprieties solely from fear to violate them. It has well been said: "The mistakes which make us men are better than the accuracies that keep us children."

YES, he went an' stole our steers,
    So, of course, he had to die;
I ain't sheddin' any tears,
      But, when I cash in—say, I
      Want to take it like that guy—
Laughin', jokin', with the rest,
      Not a whimper, not a cry,
Standin' up to meet the test
      Till we swung him clear an' high,
With his face turned toward the west!

Here's the way it looks to me;
Cattle thief's no thing to be,
But if you take up that trade,
Be the best one ever made;
If you've got a thing to do
Do it strong an' SEE IT THROUGH!

That was him! He played the game,
    Took his chances, bet his hand,
When at last the showdown came
    An' he lost, he kept his sand;
Didn't weep an' didn't pray,
    Didn't waver er repent,
Simply tossed his cards away,
    Knowin' well just what it meant.
Never claimed the deck was stacked,
    Never called the game a snide,
Acted like a man should act,
    Took his medicine—an' died!

So I say it here again,
What I think is true of men;
They should try to do what's right,
Fair an' square an' clean an' white,
But, whatever is their line,
Bad er good er foul er fine,
Let 'em go the Limit, play
Like a plunger, that's the way!

Berton Braley

RESOLVE

There are some things we should all resolve to do. What are they? Any one may make a list for himself. It would be interesting to compare it with the one here.

TO keep my health!
   To do my work!
To live!
To see to it I grow and gain and give!
Never to look behind me for an hour!
To wait in weakness and to walk in power;
But always fronting onward to the light,
Always and always facing towards the right.

Robbed, starved, defeated, fallen, wide astray—
On, with what strength I have!
Back to the way!

Charlotte Perkins Gilman

WHEN NATURE WANTS A MAN

Only melting and hammering can shape and temper steel for fine use. Only struggle and suffering can give a man the qualities that enable him to render large service to humanity. Lincoln was born in a log cabin. He split rails and read books by firelight in the evening. He became a backwoods lawyer with apparently no advantages or encouraging prospects. But all the while he had his visions, which ever became nobler; and the adversities he knew but gave him the deeper sympathy for others and the wider and steadier outlook on human problems. Thus when the supreme need arose, Lincoln was ready—harsh-visaged nature had done its work of molding and preparing a man.

WHEN nature wants to drill a man
  And thrill a man,
And skill a man,
When Nature wants to mold a man
To play the noblest part;
When she yearns with all her heart
To create so great and bold a man
That all the world shall praise—
Watch her method, watch her ways!
How she ruthlessly perfects
Whom she royally elects;
How she hammers him and hurts him
And with mighty blows converts him
Into trial shapes of clay which only Nature
  understands—
While his tortured heart is crying and he lifts
  beseeching hands!—
How she bends, but never breaks,
When his good she undertakes....
How she uses whom she chooses
And with every purpose fuses him,

By every art induces him
To try his splendor out—
Nature knows what she's about.

When Nature wants to take a man
And shake a man
And wake a man;
When Nature wants to make a man
To do the Future's will;
When she tries with all her skill
And she yearns with all her soul
To create him large and whole....
With what cunning she prepares him!
How she goads and never spares him,
How she whets him and she frets him
And in poverty begets him....
How she often disappoints
Whom she sacredly anoints,
With what wisdom she will hide him,
Never minding what betide him
Though his genius sob with slighting and his
      pride may not forget!
Bids him struggle harder yet.
Makes him lonely
So that only
God's high messages shall reach him
So that she may surely teach him
What the Hierarchy planned.
Though he may not understand
Gives him passions to command—
How remorselessly she spurs him,
With terrific ardor stirs him
When she poignantly prefers him!

When nature wants to name a man
And fame a man

And tame a man;
When Nature wants to shame a man
To do his heavenly best....
When she tries the highest test
That her reckoning may bring—
When she wants a god or king!—
How she reins him and restrains him
So his body scarce contains him
While she fires him
And inspires him!
Keeps him yearning, ever burning for a
    tantalising goal—
Lures and lacerates his soul.
Sets a challenge for his spirit,
Draws it higher when he's near it—
Makes a jungle, that he clear it;
Makes a desert, that he fear it
And subdue it if he can—
So doth Nature make a man.
Then, to test his spirit's wrath
Hurls a mountain in his path—
Puts a bitter choice before him
And relentless stands o'er him.
"Climb, or perish!" so she says...
Watch her purpose, watch her ways!

Nature's plan is wondrous kind
Could we understand her mind...
Fools are they who call her blind.
When his feet are torn and bleeding
Yet his spirit mounts unheeding,
All his higher powers speeding
Blazing newer paths and fine;
When the force that is divine
Leaps to challenge every failure and his ardor
    still is sweet

And love and hope are burning in the presence
    of defeat...
Lo, the crisis! Lo, the shout
That must call the leader out.
When the people need salvation
    Doth he come to lead the nation...
Then doth Nature show her plan
When the world has found—a man!

Angela Morgan

ORDER AND THE BEES
(From "Henry V")

We often wish that we might do some other man's work, occupy his social or political station. But such an interchange is not easy. The world is complex, and its adjustments have come from long years of experience. Each man does well to perform the tasks for which nature and training have fitted him. And instead of feeling envy toward other people, we should rejoice that all labor, however diverse, is to one great end—it makes life richer and fuller.

THEREFORE doth heaven divide
    The state of man in divers functions,
Setting endeavor in continual motion;
To which is fixéd, as an aim or butt,
Obedience: for so work the honey-bees,
Creatures that by a rule in nature teach
The act of order to a peopled kingdom.
They have a king and officers of sorts;
Where some, like magistrates, correct at home,
Others, like merchants, venture trade abroad,
Others, like soldiers, arméd in their stings,
Make boot upon the summer's velvet buds;
Which pillage they with merry march bring home
To the tent-royal of their emperor:
Who, busied in his majesty, surveys
The singing masons building roofs of gold,
The civil citizens kneading up the honey,

The poor mechanic porters crowding in
Their heavy burdens at his narrow gate,
The sad-eyed justice, with his surly hum,
Delivering o'er to executors pale
The lazy yawning drone. I this infer,
That many things, having full reference
To one consent, may work contrariously.

William Shakespeare

SELF-DEPENDENCE

One star does not ask another to adore it or amuse it; Mt. Shasta, though it towers for thousands of feet above its neighbors, does not repine that is alone or that the adjacent peaks see much that it misses under the clouds. Nature does not trouble itself about what the rest of nature is doing. But man constantly worries about other men—what they think of him, do to him, fail to emulate in him, have or secure in comparison with him. He lacks nature's inward quietude. Calmness and peace come by being self-contained.

WEARY of myself, and sick of asking
What I am, and what I ought to be,
At this vessel's prow I stand, which bears me
Forwards, forwards, o'er the starlit sea.

And a look of passionate desire
O'er the sea and to the stars I send:
"Ye who from my childhood up have calmed me,
Calm me, ah, compose me to the end!

"Ah, once more," I cried, "ye stars, ye waters,
On my heart your mighty charm renew;
Still, still let me, as I gaze upon you,
Feel my soul becoming vast like you!"

From the intense, clear, star-sown vault of heaven,
Over the lit sea's unquiet way,
In the rustling night-air came the answer:
"Wouldst thou BE as these are? LIVE as they.

"Unaffrighted by the silence round them,
Undistracted by the sights they see,
These demand not that the things without them
Yield them love, amusement, sympathy.

"And with joy the stars perform their shining,
And the sea its long, moon-silver'd roll;
For self-poised they live, nor pine with noting
All the fever of some differing soul.

"Bounded by themselves, and unregardful
In what state God's other works may be,
In their own tasks all their powers pouring,
These attain the mighty life you see."

O air-born voice! long since, severely clear,
A cry like thine in mine own heart I hear:
"Resolve to be thyself; and know that he
Who finds himself, loses his misery!"

Matthew Arnold

A LITTLE PRAYER

We should strive to bring what happiness we can to others. More still, we should strive to bring them no unhappiness. When we come to die, it is, as George Eliot once said, not our kindness or our patience or our generosity that we shall regret but our intolerance and our harshness.

THAT I may not in blindness grope,
But that I may with vision clear
Know when to speak a word of hope
Or add a little wholesome cheer.

That tempered winds may softly blow
Where little children, thinly clad,
Sit dreaming, when the flame is low,
Of comforts they have never had.

That through the year which lies ahead
   No heart shall ache, no cheek be wet,
For any word that I have said
   Or profit I have tried to get.

S.E. Kiser

A MAN'S A MAN FOR A' THAT

    It is said that once at a laird's house Burns was placed at a second table, and that this rankled in his breast and caused him to write his poem on equality. He insists that rank, wealth, and external distinctions are merely the stamp on the guinea; the man is the gold itself. Snobbishness he abhors; poverty he confesses to without hanging his head in the least; the pith of sense and the pride of worth he declares superior to any dignity thrust upon a person from the outside. In a final, prophetic mood he looks forward to the time when a democracy of square dealing shall prevail, praise shall be reserved for merit, and men the world over shall be to each other as brothers. In line 8 gowd—gold; 9, hamely—homely, commonplace; 11, gie—give; 15, sae—so; 17, birkie—fellow; 20, cuif—simpleton; 25, mak—make; 27, aboon—above; 28, mauna—must not; fa'—claim; 36, gree—prize.

I S there, for honest poverty,
  That hangs his head, and a' that?
The coward-slave, we pass him by,
    We dare be poor for a' that!
     For a' that, and a' that!
       Our toils obscure, and a' that;
      The rank is but the guinea stamp;
      The man's the gowd for a' that.

What tho' on hamely fare we dine,
   Wear hodden-gray, and a' that;
Gie fools their silks, and knaves their wine,
   A man's a man for a' that.
    For a' that, and a' that,
      Their tinsel show, and a' that;
     The honest man, tho' e'er sae poor,
      Is King o' men for a' that.

Ye see yon birkie, ca'd a lord,
    Wha struts, and stares, and a' that?
Tho' hundreds worship at his word,
    He's but a cuif for a' that:
      For a' that, and a' that,
        His riband, star, and a' that,
      The man of independent mind,
        He looks and laughs at a' that.

A prince can mak a belted knight,
    A marquis, duke, and a' that;
But an honest man's aboon his might,
    Guid faith he mauna fa' that!
      For a' that, and a' that,
        Their dignities, and a' that,
      The pith o' sense, and pride o' worth,
        Are higher rank than a' that.

Then let us pray that come it may,
    As come it will for a' that;
That sense and worth, o'er a' the earth,
    May bear the gree, and a' that.
      For a' that and a' that,
        It's coming yet, for a' that,
      That man to man the warld o'er
        Shall brothers be for a' that.

Robert Burns

LIFE AND DEATH

L IFE! I now not what though art,
  But know that thou and I must part;
And when, or how, or where we met
I own to me a secret yet.

Life! We've been long together,
Through pleasant and through cloudy weather;
'Tis hard to part when friends are dear;
Perhaps will cost a sigh, a tear;
    Then steal away, give little warning,
Choose thine own time;
Say not "Good Night" but in some brighter clime,
    Bid me "Good Morning!"

Anna Barbauld

LIFE AND DEATH

Many a man would die for wife and children, for faith, for country. But would he live for them? That, often, is the more heroic course—and the more sensible. A rich man was hiring a driver for his carriage. He asked each applicant how close he could drive to a precipice without toppling over. "One foot," "Six inches," "Three inches," ran the replies. But an Irishman declared, "Faith, and I'd keep as far away from the place as I could." "Consider yourself employed," was the rich man's comment.

SO he died for his faith. That is fine—
    More than most of us do.
But stay, can you add to that line
    That he lived for it, too?

In death he bore witness at last
    As a martyr to truth.
Did his life do the same in the past
    From the days of his youth?

It is easy to die. Men have died
    For a wish or a whim—
From bravado or passion or pride.
    Was it harder for him?

But to live: every day to live out
    All the truth that he dreamt,

78

While his friends met his conduct with doubt,
    And the world with contempt—

Was it thus that he plodded ahead,
    Never turning aside?
Then we'll talk of the life that he led—
    Never mind how he died.

Ernest H. Crosby

ON BEING READY

    At nightfall after bloody Antietam Lee's army, outnumbered and exhausted, lay with the Potomac at its back. So serious was the situation that all the subordinate officers advised retreat. But Lee, though too maimed to attack, would not leave the field save of his own volition. "If McClellan wants a battle," he declared, "he can have it." McClellan hesitated, and through the whole of the next day kept his great army idle. The effect upon the morale of the two forces, and the two governments, can be imagined.

THE man who is there with the wallop and punch
    The one who is trained to the minute,
May well be around when the trouble begins,
    But you seldom will find he is in it;
For they let him alone when they know he is there
    For any set part in the ramble,
To pick out the one who is shrinking and soft
    And not quite attuned to the scramble.

The one who is fixed for whatever they start
    Is rarely expected to prove it;
They pass him along for the next shot in sight
    Where they take a full wind-up and groove it;
For who wants to pick on a bulldog or such
    Where a quivering poodle is handy,
When he knows he can win with a kick or a brick
    With no further trouble to bandy?

Grantland Rice

TWO AT A FIRESIDE

I BUILT a chimney for a comrade old,
    I did the service not for hope or hire—
And then I traveled on in winter's cold,
    Yet all the day I glowed before the fire.

Edwin Markham

TODAY

We often lose the happiness of today by brooding over the sorrows of yesterday or fearing the troubles of tomorrow. This is exceedingly foolish. There is always some pleasure at hand; seize it, and at no time will you be without pleasure. You cannot change the past, but your spirit at this moment will in some measure shape your future. Live life, therefore, in the present tense; do not miss the joys of today.

S URE, this world is full of trouble—
    I ain't said it ain't.
Lord! I've had enough, an' double,
    Reason for complaint.
Rain an' storm have come to fret me,
    Skies were often gray;
Thorns an' brambles have beset me
    On the road—but, say,
    Ain't it fine today?

What's the use of always weepin',
    Makin' trouble last?
What's the use of always keepin'
    Thinkin' of the past?
Each must have his tribulation,
    Water with his wine.
Life it ain't no celebration.
    Trouble? I've had mine—
    But today is fine.

It's today that I am livin',
    Not a month ago,
Havin', losin', takin', givin',
    As time wills it so.
Yesterday a cloud of sorrow
    Fell across the way;
It may rain again tomorrow,
    It may rain—but, say
    Ain't it fine today!

Douglas Malloch

THE ARROW AND THE SONG

We can calculate with fair accuracy the number of miles an automobile will go in an hour. We can gauge pretty closely the amount of merchandise a given sum of money will buy. But a good deed or a kind impulse is not measurable. Their influence works in devious ways and lives on when perhaps we can see them no more.

I SHOT an arrow into the air,
    It fell to earth, I knew not where;
For, so swiftly it flew, the sight
Could not follow it in its flight.

I breathed a song into the air,
It fell to earth, I knew not where;
For who has sight so keen and strong,
That it can follow the flight of song?

Long, long afterward, in an oak
I found the arrow, still unbroke;
And the song, from beginning to end,
I found again in the heart of a friend.

Henry Wadsworth Longfellow

THE INNER LIGHT

"Thrice is he armed that hath his quarrel just,
And he but naked, though locked up in steel,
Whose conscience with injustice is corrupted,"

says Shakespeare. But not only does a clear conscience give power; it also gives light. With it we could sit at the center of the earth and yet enjoy the sunshine. Without it we live in a rayless prison.

HE that has light within his own clear breast
  May sit i' the center, and enjoy bright day:
But he that hides a dark soul and foul thoughts
Benighted walks under the midday sun;
Himself is his own dungeon.

John Milton

THE THINGS THAT HAVEN'T BEEN DONE BEFORE

It is said that if you hold a stick in front of the foremost sheep in a flock that files down a trail in the mountains, he will jump it—and that every sheep thereafter will jump when he reaches the spot, even if the stick be removed. So are many people mere unthinking imitators, blind to facts and opportunities about them. Kentucky could not be lived in by the white race until Daniel Boone built his cabin there. The air was not part of the domain of humanity till the Wright brothers made themselves birdmen.

THE things that haven't been done before,
  Those are the things to try;
Columbus dreamed of an unknown shore
  At the rim of the far-flung sky,
And his heart was bold and his faith was strong
  As he ventured in dangers new,
And he paid no heed to the jeering throng
  Or the fears of the doubting crew.

The many will follow the beaten track
  With guideposts on the way,
They live and have lived for ages back

With a chart for every day.
Someone has told them it's safe to go
    On the road he has traveled o'er,
And all that they ever strive to know
    Are the things that were known before.

A few strike out, without map or chart,
    Where never a man has been,
From the beaten paths they draw apart
    To see what no man has seen.
There are deeds they hunger alone to do;
    Though battered and bruised and sore,
They blaze the path for the many, who
    Do nothing not done before.

The things that haven't been done before
    Are the tasks worth while today;
Are you one of the flock that follows, or
    Are you one that shall lead the way?
Are you one of the timid souls that quail
    At the jeers of a doubting crew,
Or dare you, whether you win or fail,
    Strike out for a goal that's new?

Edgar A. Guest

THE HAS-BEENS

I READ the papers every day, and oft encounter tales which show there's hope for every jay who in life's battles fails. I've just been reading of a gent who joined the has-been ranks—at fifty years without a cent or credit at the banks. But undismayed he buckled down, refusing to be beat, and captured fortune and renown; he's now on Easy Street. Men say that fellows down and out ne'er leave that rocky track, but facts will show, beyond a doubt, that has-beens do come back. I know, for I who write this rhyme, when forty-odd years old, was down and out, without a dime, my whiskers full of mold. By black disaster I was trounced until it jarred my spine; I was a failure so pronounced I didn't need a sign. And after I had soaked my coat, I said (at forty-three), "I'll see if I can catch the goat that has escaped from me." I labored hard; I strained my dome, to do my daily grind, until in triumph I came home, my billy-goat behind. And any man who still has health may with the winners stack, and have a chance at fame and wealth—for has-beens do come back.

Walt Mason

WISHING

Horace Greeley said that no one need fear the editor who indulged in diatribes against the prevalence of polygamy in Utah, but that malefactors had better look out when an editor took up his pen against abuses in his own city. We all tend to begin reforms too far away from home. The man who wishes improvement strongly enough to set to work on himself is the man who will obtain results.

DO you wish the world were better?
    Let me tell you what to do.
Set a watch upon your actions,
    Keep them always straight and true.
Rid your mind of selfish motives,
    Let your thoughts be clean and high.
You can make a little Eden
    Of the sphere you occupy.

Do you wish the world were wiser?
    Well, suppose you make a start,
By accumulating wisdom
    In the scrapbook of your heart;
Do not waste one page on folly;
    Live to learn, and learn to live.
If you want to give men knowledge
    You must get it, ere you give.

Do you wish the world were happy?
  Then remember day by day
Just to scatter seeds of kindness
  As you pass along the way,
For the pleasures of the man
  May be ofttimes traced to one.
As the hand that plants an acorn
  Shelters armies from the sun.

Ella Wheeler Wilcox

AWARENESS

A man must keep a keen sense of the drift and significance of what he is engaged in if he is to make much headway. Yet many human beings are so sunk in the routine of their work that they fail to realize what it is all for. A man who was tapping with a hammer the wheels of a railroad train remarked that he had been at the job for 27 years. "What do you do when a wheel doesn't sound right?" a passenger inquired. The man was taken aback. "I never found one that sounded that way," said he.

G OD—let me be aware.
  Let me not stumble blindly down the ways,
Just getting somehow safely through the days,
Not even groping for another hand,
Not even wondering why it all was planned,
Eyes to the ground unseeking for the light,
Soul never aching for a wild-winged flight,
Please, keep me eager just to do my share.
God—let me be aware.

God—let me be aware.
Stab my soul fiercely with others' pain,
Let me walk seeing horror and stain.
Let my hands, groping, find other hands.
Give me the heart that divines, understands.
Give me the courage, wounded, to fight.
Flood me with knowledge, drench me in light.

Please—keep me eager just to do my share.
God—let me be aware.

Miriam Teichner

ONE OF THESE DAYS

The worst fault in a hound is to run counter—to follow the trail backward, not forward. Is the fault less when men are guilty of it? Behind us is much that we have found to be faithless, cruel, or unpleasant. Why go back to that? Why not go forward to the things we really desire?

S AY! Let's forget it! Let's put it aside!
Life is so large and the world is so wide.
Days are so short and there's so much to do,
What if it was false—there's plenty that's true.
Now and forever, so what do you say?
All of the bitter words said may be praise
One of these days.

Say! Let's forget it! Let's wipe off the slate,
Find something better to cherish than hate.
There's so much good in the world that we've had,
Let's strike a balance and cross off the bad.
Say! Let's forgive it, whatever it be,
Let's not be slaves when we ought to be free.
We shall be walking in sunshiny ways
One of these days.

Say! Let's not mind it! Let's smile it away,
Bring not a withered rose from yesterday;
Flowers are so fresh from the wayside and wood,
Sorrows are blessings but half understood.
Say! Let's not mind it, however it seems,
Hope is so sweet and holds so many dreams;
All of the sere fields with blossoms shall blaze
One of these days.

Say! Let's not take it so sorely to heart!
Hates may be friendships just drifted apart,
Failure be genius not quite understood,
We could all help folks so much if we would
Say! Let's get closer to somebody's side,
See what his dreams are and learn how he tried,
See if our scoldings won't give way to praise
One of these days.

Say! Let's not wither! Let's branch out and rise
Out of the byways and nearer the skies.
Let's spread some shade that's refreshing and deep
Where some tired traveler may lie down and sleep.
Say! Let's not tarry! Let's do it right now;
So much to do if we just find out how!
We may not be here to help folks or praise
One of these days.

James W. Foley

GOD

We often think people shallow, think them incapable of anything serious or profound, because their work is humdrum and their speech trivial. Such a judgment is unfair, since that part of our own life that shows itself to others is superficial likewise, though we are conscious that within us is much that it does not reveal.

I THINK about God.
   Yet I talk of small matters.
Now isn't it odd
   How my idle tongue chatters!
Of quarrelsome neighbors,
   Fine weather and rain,
Indifferent labors,
   Indifferent pain,
Some trivial style

Fashion shifts with a nod.
And yet all the while
I am thinking of God.

Gamaliel Bradford

MY TRIUMPH

The poet, looking back upon the hopes he has cherished, perceives that he has fallen far short of achieving them. The songs he has sung are less sweet than those he has dreamed of singing; the wishes he has wrought into facts are less noble than those that are yet unfulfilled. But he looks forward to the time when all that he desires for humankind shall yet come to pass. The praise will not be his; it will belong to others. Still, he does not envy those who are destined to succeed where he failed. Rather does he rejoice that through them his hopes for the race will be realized. And he is happy that by longing for just such a triumph he shares in it—he makes it his triumph.

L ET the thick curtain fall;
I better know than all
How little I have gained,
How vast the unattained.

Not by the page word-painted
Let life be banned or sainted:
Deeper than written scroll
The colors of the soul.

Sweeter than any sung
My songs that found no tongue,
Nobler than any fact
My wish that failed to act.

Others shall sing the song,
Others shall right the wrong—
Finish what I begin,
And all I fail of win.

What matter, I or they?
Mine or another's day,
So the right word be said
And life the sweeter made.

Hail to the coming singers!
Hail to the brave light-bringers!
Forward I reach and share
All that they sing and dare.

The airs of heaven blow o'er me;
A glory shines before me
Of what mankind shall be—
Pure, generous, brave, and free.

A dream of man and woman
Diviner but still human,
Solving the riddle old,
Shaping the Age of Gold!

The love of God and neighbor;
An equal-handed labor;
The richer life, where beauty
Walks hand in hand with duty.

Ring, bells in unreared steeples,
The joy of unborn peoples!
Sound, trumpets far off blown,
Your triumph is my own.

Parcel and part of all,
I keep the festival,
Fore-reach the good to be,
And share the victory.

I feel the earth move sunward,
I join the great march onward,
And take, by faith, while living,
My freehold of thanksgiving.

John Greenleaf Whittier

TO ALTHEA FROM PRISON

In the great Civil War in England between the Puritans and Charles the First, the author of this poem sacrificed everything in the royal cause. The cause was defeated and Lovelace was imprisoned. In these stanzas, he makes the most of his gloomy situation and sings the joys of various kinds of freedom. First is the freedom brought by love, when his sweetheart speaks to him through the grate of the dungeon. Second is the freedom brought by the recollection of good fellowship, when tried and true comrades took their wine straight—"with no allaying Thames." Third is the freedom brought by remembrance of the king for whom he was suffering. Finally comes the passionate and heroic assertion that though the body of a man may be confined, nevertheless his spirit can remain free and chainless.

WHEN Love with unconfinéd wings
    Hovers within my gates,
And my divine Althea brings
    To whisper at the grates;
When I lie tangled in her hair
    And fetter'd to her eye,
The Gods that wanton in the air
    Know no such liberty.

When flowing cups run swiftly round
    With no allaying Thames,
Our careless heads with roses bound,
    Our hearts with loyal flames;
When thirsty grief in wine we steep,
    When healths and draughts go free,
Fishes that tipple in the deep
    Know no such liberty.

When (like committed linnets) I
    With shriller throat shall sing
The sweetness, mercy, majesty
    And glories of my King;
When I shall voice aloud how good
    He is, how great should be,
Enlargéd winds, that curl the flood,
    Know no such liberty.

Stone walls do not a prison make,
    Nor iron bars a cage;
Minds innocent and quiet take
    That for an hermitage;
If I have freedom in my love
    And in my soul am free,
Angels alone, that soar above,
    Enjoy such liberty.

Richard Lovelace

GRIEF

Shakespeare says: "I can easier teach twenty what were good to be done than be one of the twenty to follow mine own teaching." This is especially true regarding grief or affliction. "Man was born unto trouble, as the sparks fly upward," but we bid other people bear their sorrows manfully; we should therefore bear ours with equal courage.

UPON this trouble shall I whet my life
    As 'twere a dulling knife;
Bade I my friend be brave?
I shall still braver be.
No man shall say of me,
"Others he saved, himself he cannot save."
But swift and fair
As the Primeval word that smote the night—
"Let there be light!"
Courage shall leap from me, a gallant sword

To rout the enemy and all his horde,
Cleaving a kingly pathway through despair.

Angela Morgan

THE RECTIFYING YEARS

Time brings the deeper understanding that clears up our misconceptions; it shows us the error of our hates; it dispels our worries and our fears; it allays the grief that seemed too poignant to be borne.

YES, things are more or less amiss;
   Today it's that, tomorrow this;
Yet with so much that's out of whack,
Life does not wholly jump the track
Because, since matters move along,
No *one* thing's always *staying* wrong.
So heed not failures, losses, fears,
But trust the rectifying years.

What we shall have's not what we've got;
Our pains don't linger in one spot—
They skip about; the seesaw's end
That's up will mighty soon descend;
You've looked at bacon? Life's like that—
A streak of lean, a streak of fat.
Change, like a sky that clouds, that clears,
Hangs o'er the rectifying years.

Uneven things not leveled down
Are somehow simply got aroun';
The sting is taken from offense;
The evil has its recompense;
The broken heart is knit again;
The baffled longing knows not pain;
Wrong fades and trouble disappears
Before the rectifying years.

Then envy, hate towards man or class
Should from your sinful nature pass.
Though others hold a higher place
Or have more power or wealth or grace,
The best of them, be sure, cannot
Escape the common human lot;
So many smiles, so many tears
Come with the rectifying years.

St. Clair Adams

TO THOSE WHO FAIL

We too often praise the man who wins just because he wins; the plaudits and laurels of victory are the unthinking crowd's means of estimating success. But the vanquished may have fought more nobly than the victor; he may have done his best against hopeless odds. As Addison makes Cato say,

"'Tis not in mortals to command success,
But we'll do more, Sempronius—we'll deserve it."

"ALL honor to him who shall win the prize,"
    The world has cried for a thousand years;
But to him who tries, and who fails and dies,
I give great honor and glory and tears;

Give glory and honor and pitiful tears
To all who fail in their deeds sublime;
Their ghosts are many in the van of years,
They were born with Time, in advance of Time.

Oh, great is the hero who wins a name,
But greater many and many a time
Some pale-faced fellow who dies in shame,
And lets God finish the thoughts sublime.

And great is the man with a sword undrawn,
And good is the man who refrains from wine;

93

But the man who fails and yet still fights on,
Lo, he is the twin-born brother of mine.

Joaquin Miller

OPENING PARADISE

We appreciate even the common things of life if we are denied them.

SEE the wretch, that long has tost
On the thorny bed of Pain,
At length repair his vigor lost,
And breathe and walk again:
The meanest flow'r'et of the vale,
The simplest note that swells the gale,
The common Sun, the air, and skies,
To him are opening Paradise.

Thomas Gray

TO THE MEN WHO LOSE

When Captain Scott's ill-fated band, after reaching the South Pole, was struggling through the cold and storms back towards safety, the strength of Evans, one of the men, became exhausted. He had done his best but in vain. Now, he did not wish to imperil his companions, already sorely tried. At a halting-place, therefore, he left them and, staggering out into a blizzard, perished alone. It was a failure, yes; but was it not also magnificent success?

HERE'S to the men who lose!
What though their work be e'er so nobly planned,
And watched with zealous care,
No glorious halo crowns their efforts grand,
Contempt is failure's share.

Here's to the men who lose!
If triumph's easy smile our struggles greet,
Courage is easy then;

The king is he who, after fierce defeat,
    Can up and fight again.

Here's to the men who lose!
The ready plaudits of a fawning world
    Ring sweet in victor's ears;
The vanquished's banners never are unfurled—
    For them there sound no cheers.

Here's to the men who lose!
The touchstone of true worth is not success;
    There is a higher test—
Though fate may darkly frown, onward to press,
    And bravely do one's best.

Here's to the men who lose!
It is the vanquished's praises that I sing,
    And this is the toast I choose:
"A hard-fought failure is a noble thing;
    Here's to the men who lose!"

Anonymous

IT MAY BE

Many, many are the human struggles in which we can lend no aid. But if we cannot help, at least we need not hinder.

IT may be that you cannot stay
    To lend a friendly hand to him
Who stumbles on the slippery way,
    Pressed by conditions hard and grim;
It may be that you dare not heed
    His call for help, because you lack
The strength to lift him, but you need
    Not push him back.

It may be that he has not won
The right to hope for your regard;
He may in folly have begun
The course that he has found so hard;
It may be that your fingers bleed,
That Fortune turns a bitter frown
Upon your efforts, but you need
Not kick him down.

S. E. Kiser

LIFE

In life is necessarily much monotony, sameness. But our triumph may lie in putting richness and meaning into routine that apprarently lacks them.

FORENOON and afternoon and night—Forenoon,
And afternoon, and night—Forenoon, and —what!
The empty song repeats itself. No more?
Yea, that is Life: make this forenoon sublime,
This afternoon a psalm, this night a prayer,
And Time is conquered, and thy crown is won.

Edward Rowland Sill

THE GRUMPY GUY

When students came, full of ambition, to the great scientist, Agassiz, he gave them each a fish and told them to find out what they could about it. They went to work and in a day or two were ready for their report. But Agassiz didn't come round. To kill time they went to work again, observed, dissected, conjectured, and when at the end of a fortnight Agassiz finally appeared, they felt that their knowledge was really exhaustive. The master's brief comment was that they had made a fair beginning, and again he left. They then fell to in earnest and after weeks and months of investigation declared that a fish was the most fascinating of studies. If our interest in life fails, it is not from material to work on. No two leaves are alike, not two human beings are alike, and if we are discerning, the attraction of any one of them is infinite.

THE Grumpy Guy was feeling blue; the Grumpy Guy
was glum;

The Grumpy Guy with baleful eye took Misery for a
    chum.
He hailed misfortunes as his pals, and murmured, "Let
    'em come!

"Oh, what's the blooming use?" he yelped, his face an
    angry red,
"When everything's been thought before and everything's
    been said?
And what's a Grumpy Guy to do except to go to bed?

"And where's the joy the poets sing, the merriment and
    fun?
How can one start a thing that's new when everything's
    begun?—
When everything's been planned before and everything's
    been done?—

"When everything's been dreamed before and everything's
    been sought?
When everything that ever ran has, so to speak, been
    caught?—
When every game's been played before and every battle
    fought?"

I started him at solitaire, a fooling, piffling game.
He played it ninety-seven hours and failed to find it tame.
In all the times he dealt the cards no two games were the
    same.

He never tumbled to its tricks nor mastered all its curves.
He grunted, "Well, this takes the cake, the pickles and the
    preserves!
Its infinite variety is getting on my nerves."

"Its infinite variety!" I scoffed. "Just fifty-two
Poor trifling bits of pasteboard!—their combinations few

Compared to what there is in man!—the poorest!—even
   you!

"Variety! You'll never find in forty-seven decks
One tenth of the variety found in the gentler sex.
Card combinations are but frills to hang around their
   necks.

"The sun won't rise tomorrow as it came to us today.
'Twill be older, we'll be older, and to Time this debt we
   pay.
For nothing can repeat itself, for nothing knows the way."

Then the Grumpy Guy was silent as a miser hoarding
   pelf.
He knew 'twas time to put his grouch away upon the
   shelf.
And so he did.—You see, I was just talking to myself!

Griffith Alexander

THE FIGHTER

If life were all easy, we should degenerate into weaklings—into human
mush. It is the fighting spirit that makes us strong. Nor do any of us lack for a
chance to exercise this spirit. Struggle is everywhere; as Kearny said at Fair Oaks,
"There is lovely fighting along the whole line."

I FIGHT a battle every day
   Against discouragement and fear;
Some foe stands always in my way,
      The path ahead is never clear!
I must forever be on guard
      Against the doubts that skulk along;
I get ahead by fighting hard,
      But fighting keeps my spirit strong.

I hear the croakings of Despair,
  The dark predictions of the weak;
I find myself pursued by Care,
  No matter what the end I seek;
My victories are small and few,
  It matters not how hard I strive;
Each day the fight begins anew,
  But fighting keeps my hopes alive.

My dreams are spoiled by circumstance,
  My plans are wrecked by Fate or Luck;
Some hour, perhaps, will bring my chance,
  But that great hour has never struck;
My progress has been slow and hard,
  I've had to climb and crawl and swim,
Fighting for every stubborn yard,
  But I have kept in fighting trim.

I have to fight my doubts away,
  And be on guard against my fears;
The feeble croaking of Dismay
  Has been familiar through the years;
My dearest plans keep going wrong,
  Events combine to thwart my will,
But fighting keeps my spirit strong,
  And I am undefeated still!

S. E. Kiser

TO YOUTH AFTER PAIN

Since pain is the lot of all, we cannot hope to escape it. Since only through pain can we come into true and helpful sympathy with others, we should not wish to escape it.

WHAT if this year has given
  Grief that some year must bring,
What if it hurt your joyous youth,

Crippled your laughter's wing?
You always knew it was coming,
  Coming to all, to you,
They always said there was suffering—
  Now it is done, come through.

Even if you have blundered,
  Even if you have sinned,
Still is the steadfast arch of the sky
  And the healing veil of the wind...
And after only a little,
  A little of hurt and pain,
You shall have the web of your own old dreams
  Wrapping your heart again.

Only your heart can pity
  Now, where it laughed and passed,
Now you can bend to comfort men,
  One with them all at last,
You shall have back your laughter,
  You shall have back your song,
Only the world is your brother now,
  Only your soul is strong!

Margaret Widdemer

CAN'T

A great achieving soul will not clog itself with a cowardly thought or a cowardly watchword. Cardinal Richelieu in Bulwer-Lytton's play declares:

"In the lexicon of youth, which fate reserves
For a bright manhood, there is no such word
As 'fail.'"

"Impossible," Napoleon is quoted as saying, "is a word found only in the dictionary of fools."

*C*AN'T is the worst word that's written or spoken;
    Doing more harm here than slander and lies;
On it is many a strong spirit broken,
    And with it many a good purpose dies.
It springs from the lips of the thoughtless each morning
    And robs us of courage we need through the day:
It rings in our ears like a timely sent warning
    And laughs when we falter and fall by the way.

Can't is the father of feeble endeavor,
    The parent of terror and half-hearted work;
It weakens the efforts of artisans clever,
    And makes of the toiler an indolent shirk.
It poisons the soul of the man with a vision,
    It stifles in infancy many a plan;
It greets honest toiling with open derision
    And mocks at the hopes and the dreams of a man.

Can't is a word none should speak without blushing;
    To utter it should be a symbol of shame;
Ambition and courage it daily is crushing;
    It blights a man's purpose and shortens his aim.
Despise it with all of your hatred of error;
    Refuse it the lodgment it seeks in your brain;
Arm against it as a creature of terror,
    And all that you dream of you some day shall gain.

Can't is the word that is foe to ambition,
    An enemy ambushed to shatter your will;
Its prey is forever the man with a mission
    And bows but to courage and patience and skill.
Hate it, with hatred that's deep and undying,
    For once it is welcomed 'twill break any man;
Whatever the goal you are seeking, keep trying
    And answer this demon by saying: *I can.*"

Edgar A. Guest

THE STRUGGLE

We all dream of being St. Georges and fighting dragons amid glamor and glory and the applause of the world. But our real fights are mostly commonplace, routine battles, where no great victory is ours at the end of the day. To persist in them requires quiet strength and unfaltering courage.

DID you ever want to take your two bare hands
  And choke out of the world your big success?
Beat, torn fists bleeding, pathways rugged, grand,
  By sheer brute strength and bigness, nothing less?
So at the last, triumphant, battered, strong,
  You might gaze down on what you choked and beat,
And say, "Ah, world, you've wrought to do me wrong;
  And thus have I accepted my defeat."

Have you ever dreamed of virile deeds, and vast,
  And then come back from dreams with wobbly knees,
To find your way (the braver vision past),
  By picking meekly at typewriter keys;
By bending o'er a ledger, day by day,
  By some machine-like drudging? No great woe
To grapple with. Slow, painful is the way,
  And still, the bravest fight and conquer so.

Miriam Teichner

HOLD FAST

A football coach who told his players that their rivals were too strong for them would be seeking a new position the next year. If the opposing team is formidable, he says so; if his men have their work cut out for them, he admits it; but he mentions these things as incitements to effort. Merely saying of victory that it can be won is among the surest ways of winning it.

WHEN you're nearly drowned in trouble, and the
  world is dark as ink;
When you feel yourself a-sinking 'neath the strain,

And you think, "I've got to holler 'Help!'" just take another
    breath
  And pretend you've lost your voice—and can't complain
    (That's the idea!)
  Pretend you've lost your voice and can't complain!

When the future glowers at you like a threatening thunder
    cloud,
  Just grit your teeth and bend your head and say:
"It's dark and disagreeable and I can't help feeling blue,
  But there's coming sure as fate a brighter day!"
    (Say it slowly!)
  "But there's coming sure as fate a brighter day!"

You have bluffed your way through ticklish situations;
    that I know.
  You are looking aback on troubles past and gone;
Now, turn the tables, and as you have fought and won
    before,
  Just BLUFF YOURSELF to keep on holding on!
    (Try it once.)
  Just bluff YOURSELF to keep on—holding on.

Don't worry if the roseate hues of life are faded out,
  Bend low before the storm and wait awhile.
The pendulum is bound to swing again and you will find
  That you have not forgotten how to smile.
    (That's the truth!)
  That you have not forgotten how to smile.

Everard Jack Appleton

WILL

    Warren Hastings resolved in his boyhood that he would be the owner of the estate known as Daylesford. This was the one great purpose that unified his varied and far-reaching activities. Admire him or not, we must at least praise his pluck in holding to his purpose—a purpose he ultimately attained.

YOU will be what you will to be;
  Let failure find its false content
In that poor word "environment,"
  But spirit scorns it, and is free.

  It masters time, it conquers space
It cows that boastful trickster Chance,
And bids the tyrant Circumstance
  Uncrown and fill a servant's place.

  The human Will, that force unseen,
The offspring of a deathless Soul,
Can hew the way to any goal,
  Though walls of granite intervene.

  Be not impatient in delay,
But wait as one who understands;
When spirit rises and commands
  The gods are ready to obey.

  The river seeking for the sea
Confronts the dam and precipice,
Yet knows it cannot fail or miss;
  You will be what you will to be!

Ella Wheeler Wilcox

THE GAME

Lessing said that if God should come to him with truth in one hand and the never-ending pursuit of truth in the other, and should offer him his choice, he would humbly and reverently take the pursuit of truth. Perhaps it is best that finite beings should not attain infinite success. But however remote that for which they seek or strive, they may by their diligence and generosity make the very effort to secure it noble. In doing this they earn, as Pope tells us, a truer commendation than success itself could bring them. "Act well thy part; there all the honor lies."

L ET'S play it out—this little game called Life,
   Where we are listed for so brief a spell;
Not just to win, amid the tumult rife,
   Or where acclaim and gay applauses swell;
Nor just to conquer where some one must lose,
   Or reach the goal whatever be the cost;
For there are other, better ways to choose,
   Though in the end the battle may be lost.

Let's play it out as if it were a sport
   Wherein the game is better than the goal,
And never mind the detailed "score's" report
   Of errors made, if each with dauntless soul
But stick it out until the day is done,
   Not wasting fairness for success or fame,
So when the battle has been lost or won,
   The world at least can say: "He played the game."

Let's play it out—this little game called Work,
   Or War or Love or what part each may draw;
Play like a man who scorns to quit or shirk
   Because the break may carry some deep flaw;
Nor simply holding that the goal is all
   That keeps the player in the contest staying;
But stick it out from curtain rise to fall,
   As if the game itself were worth the playing.

Grantland Rice

A GOOD NAME

We should respect the good name of other people and should safeguard our own by a high sense of honor. At the close of the Civil War a representative of an insurance company offered Robert F. Lee the presidency of the firm at a salary of $50,000 a year. Lee replied that while he wished to earn his living, he doubted whether his services would be worth so large a sum. "We don't want your services," the man interrupted; "we want your name." "That," said Lee, quietly, "is not for sale." He accepted, instead, the presidency of a college at $1,500 a year.

GOOD name in man and woman, dear my lord,
Is the immediate jewel of their souls:
Who steals my purse steals trash; 'tis something, nothing;
'Twas mine, 'tis his, and has been slave to thousands;
But he that filches from me my good name
Robs me of that which not enriches him,
And makes me poor indeed.

William Shakespeare

SWELLITIS

A certain employer of large numbers of people makes it a principle to praise none of them, not because they are undeserving and not because he dislikes to commend, but because experience has taught him that usually the praise goes to the head of the recipient, both impairing his work and making it harder for others to associate with him. A good test of a man is his way of taking commendation. He may, even while grateful, be stirred to humility that he has not done better still and may resolve to accomplish more. Or imitating the frog who wished to look like an ox, he may swell and swell until—figuratively speaking—he bursts.

SOMEBODY said he'd done it well,
And presto! his head began to swell;
Bigger and bigger the poor thing grew—
A wonder it didn't split in two.
In size a balloon could scarcely match it;
He needed a fishing-pole to scratch it—
But six and a half was the size of his hat,
And it rattled around on his head at that!

"Good work," somebody chanced to say,
And his chest swelled big as a load of hay.
About himself, like a rooster, he crowed;
Of his wonderful work he bragged and blowed.
He marched around with a peacock strut;
Gigantic to him was the figure he cut—
But he wore a very small-sized suit,
And loosely it hung on him, to boot!

HE was the chap who made things hum!
HE was the drumstick and the drum!
HE was the shirt bosom and the starch!
HE was the keystone in the arch!
HE was the axis of the earth!
Nothing existed before his birth!
But when he was off from work a day,
Nobody knew that he was away!

This is a fact that is sad to tell:
It's the empty head that is bound to swell;
It's the lightweight fellow who soars to the skies
And bursts like a bubble before your eyes.
A big man is humbled by honest praise,
And tries to think of all the ways
To improve his work and do it well—
But a little man starts of himself to yell!

Joseph Morris

CARES

To those who are wearied, fretted, and worried, there is no physician like nature. When our nerves are frazzled and our sleep is unrefreshing, we can find no better antidote than the solitude of hills, streams, and tranquil stars. That man lays up for himself resources of strength who now and then exchanges the ledger for green leaves, the factory for wild flowers, business for brook-croon and bird-song.

THE little cares that fretted me
    I lost them yesterday
Among the fields above the sea,
    Among the winds at play;
Among the lowing of the herds,
    The rustling of the trees,
Among the singing of the birds,
    The humming of the bees.

The foolish fears of what may happen.
   I cast them all away
Among the clover-scented grass,
   Among the new-mown hay;
Among the husking of the corn
   Where drowsy poppies nod,
Where ill thoughts die and good are born
   Out in the fields with God.

Elizabeth Barrett Browning

FAITH

Any one who has ridden across the continent on a train must marvel at the faith and imagination of the engineers who constructed the road—the topographical advantages seized, the grades made easy of ascent, the curves and straight stretches planned, the tunnels so carefully calculated that workers beginning on opposite sides of a mountain met in the middle—and all this visualized and thought out before the actual work was begun. Faith has such foresight, such courage, where it toils actively or can merely bide its time.

THE treetop high above the barren field,
   Rising beyond the night's gray folds of mist,
Rests stirless where the upper air is sealed
   To perfect silence, by the faint moon kissed.
But the low branches, drooping to the ground,
   Sway to and fro, as sways funereal plume,
While from their restless depths low whispers sound:
   "We fear, we fear the darkness and the gloom;
   Dim forms beneath us pass and reappear,
   And mournful tongues are menacing us here."

Then from the topmost bough falls calm reply:
   "Hush, hush, I see the coming of the morn;
Swiftly the silent night is passing by,
   And in her bosom rosy Dawn is borne.
   'Tis but your own dim shadows that ye see,
   'Tis but your own low moans that trouble ye."

So Life stands, with a twilight world around;
    Faith turned serenely to the steadfast sky,
Still answering the heart that sweeps the ground
    Sobbing in fear, and tossing restlessly—
      "Hush, hush! The Dawn breaks o'er the Eastern sea,
    'Tis but thine own dim shadow troubling thee."

Edward Rowland Sill

PLAYING THE GAME

We all like the good sport—the man who plays fair and courteously and with every ounce of his energy, even when the game is going against him.

LIFE is a game with a glorious prize,
    If we can only play it right.
It is give and take, build and break,
    And often it ends in a fight;
But he surely wins who honestly tries
    (Regardless of wealth or fame),
He can never despair who plays it fair—
    How are you playing the game?

Do you wilt and whine, if you fail to win
    In the manner you think your due?
Do you sneer at the man in case that he can
    And does, do better than you?
Do you take your rebuffs with a knowing grin?
    Do you laugh tho' you pull up lame?
Does your faith hold true when the whole world's blue?
    How are you playing the game?

Get into the thick of it—wade in, boys!
    Whatever your cherished goal;
Brace up your will till your pulses thrill,
    And you dare—to your very soul!
Do something more than make a noise;

Let your purpose leap into flame
As you plunge with a cry, "I shall do or die,"
Then you will be playing the game.

Anonymous

GLADNESS

We all have an inner light that can shine forth and bring us joy.

THE world has brought not anything
To make me glad today!
The swallow had a broken wing,
And after all my journeying
There was no water in the spring—
My friend has said me nay.
But yet somehow I needs must sing
As on a luckier day.

Dusk falls as gray as any tear,
There is no hope in sight!
But something in me seems so fair,
That like a star I needs must wear
A safety made of shining air
Between me and the night.
Such inner weavings do I wear
All fashioned of delight!

I need not for these robes of mine
The loveliness of earth,
But happenings remote and fine
Like threads of dreams will blow and shine
In gossamer and crystalline
And I was glad from birth.
So even while my eyes repine,
My heart is clothed in mirth.

Anna Hempstead Branch

THE RAINBOW

Our lives are not a hodgepodge of separate experiences, though they sometimes seem so. They are held together by simple things which we behold again and again with the same emotions. Thus the man is what the boy has been; the tree is inclined in the precise direction the twig was bent.

M Y heart leaps up when I behold
   A rainbow in the sky:
So was it when my life began;
So is it now I am a man;
So be it when I shall grow old
   Or let me die!
The Child is father of the Man;
And I could wish my days to be
Bound each to each by natural piety.

William Wordsworth

THE FIRM OF GRIN AND BARRETT

It has been said that when disaster overtakes us we can do one of two things—we can grin and bear it, or we needn't grin. The spirit that keeps a smile on our faces when our burden is heaviest is the spirit that will win in the long run. Many men know how to take success quietly. The real test of a man is the way he takes failure.

N O financial throe volcanic
   Ever yet was known to scare it;
Never yet was any panic
   Scared the firm of Grin and Barrett.
From the flurry and the fluster,
   From the ruin and the crashes,
They arise in brighter luster,
   Like the phoenix from his ashes.
When the banks and corporations
   Quake with fear, they do not share it;
Smiling through all perturbations

Goes the firm of Grin and Barrett.
   Grin and Barrett,
   Who can scare it?
Scare the firm of Grin and Barrett?

When the tide-sweep of reverses
   Smites them, firm they stand and dare it
Without wailings, tears, or curses,
   This stout firm of Grin and Barrett.
Even should their house go under
   In the flood and inundation,
Calm they stand amid the thunder
   Without noise or demonstration.
And, when sackcloth is the fashion,
   With a patient smile they wear it,
Without petulance or passion,
   This old firm of Grin and Barrett.
      Grin and Barrett,
      Who can scare it?
Scare the firm of Grin and Barrett?

When the other firms show dizziness,
   Here's a house that does not share it.
Wouldn't you like to join the business?
   Join the firm of Grin and Barrett?
Give your strength that does not murmur,
And you've joined a house that's firmer
   Than the old rock of Gibraltar
They have won a good prosperity;
   Why not join the firm and share it?
Step, young fellow, with celerity;
   Join the firm of Grin and Barrett.
      Grin and Barrett,
      Who can scare it?
Scare the firm of Grin and Barrett?

Sam Walter Foss

CHALLENGE

Napoleon is reported to have complained of the English that they didn't have sense enough to know when they were beaten. Even if defeat is unmistakable, it need not be final. A battle may be lost but the campaign won; a campaign lost but the war won.

L IFE, I challenge you to try me,
  Doom me to unending pain;
Stay my hand, becloud my vision,
   Break my heart and then—again.

Shatter every dream I've cherished,
  Fill my heart with ruthless fear;
Follow every smile that cheers me
   With a bitter, blinding tear.

Thus I dare you; you can try me,
  Seek to make me cringe and moan,
Still my unbound soul defies you,
   I'll withstand you—and, alone!

Jean Nette

YOUR MISSION

One of the most often heard of sentences is "I don't know what I'm to do in the world." Yet very few people are ever for a moment out of something to do, especially if they do not insist on climbing to the top of the pole and waving the flag but are willing to steady the pole while somebody else climbs.

I F you cannot on the ocean
  Sail among the swiftest fleet,
Rocking on the highest billows,
   Laughing at the storms you meet;
You can stand among the sailors,
  Anchored yet within the bay,
You can lend a hand to help them
   As they launch their boats away.

If you are too weak to journey
    Up the mountain, steep and high,
You can stand within the valley
    While the multitudes go by;
You can chant in happy measure
    As they slowly pass along—
Though they may forget the singer,
    They will not forget the song.

·   ·   ·   ·   ·   ·   ·

If you cannot in the harvest
    Garner up the richest sheaves,
Many a grain, both ripe and golden,
    Oft the careless reaper leaves;
Go and glean among the briars
    Growing rank against the wall,
For it may be that their shadow
    Hides the heaviest grain of all.

If you cannot in the conflict
    Prove yourself a soldier true;
If, where fire and smoke are thickest,
    There's not work for you to do;
When the battlefield is silent,
    You can go with careful tread;
You can bear away the wounded,
    You can cover up the dead.

Do not then stand idly waiting
    For some greater work to do;
Fortune is a lazy goddess,
    She will never come to you;
Go and toil in any vineyard,
    Do not fear to do and dare.
If you want a field of labor
    You can find it anywhere.

Ellen M. H. Gates

114

VICTORY

To fail is not a disgrace; the disgrace lies in not trying. In his old age Sir Walter Scott found that a publishing firm he was connected with was heavily in debt. He refused to take advantage of the bankruptcy law and sat down with his pen to make good the deficit. Though he wore out his life in the struggle and did not live to see the debt entirely liquidated, he died an honored and honorable man.

I CALL no fight a losing fight
   If, fighting, I have gained some straight new
     strength;
If, fighting, I turned ever toward the light,
All unallied with forces of the night;
If, beaten, quivering, I could say at length:
"I did no deed that needs to be unnamed;
I fought—and lost—and I am unashamed."

Miram Teichner

TIMES GO BY TURNS

One of the greatest blessings in life is alteration. The ins become outs, the outs ins; the ups become downs, the downs ups; and so on—and it is better so. We must not get too highly elated at success, for life is not all success. We must not grow too downcast from failure, for life is not all failure.

THE lopped tree in time may grow again,
   Most naked plants renew both fruit and flower;
The sorriest wight may find release of pain,
   The driest soil suck in some moistening shower;
Time goes by turns, and chances change by course,
   From foul to fair, from better hap to worse.

The sea of Fortune doth not ever flow;
   She draws her favors to the lowest ebb;
Her tides have equal times to come and go;
   Her loom doth weave the fine and coarsest web;
No joy so great but runneth to an end,
   No hap so hard but may in fine amend.

Not always fall of leaf, nor ever Spring;
    Not endless night, yet not eternal day;
The saddest birds a season find to sing;
    The roughest storm a calm may soon allay.
Thus, with succeeding turns God tempereth all,
    That man may hope to rise, yet fear to fall.

A chance may win that by mischance was lost;
    That net that holds no great takes little fish;
In some things all, in all things none are crost;
    Few all they need, but none have all they wish.
Unmingled joys here to man befall;
    Who least, hath some; who most, hath never all.

Robert Southwell

TODAY

The past did not behold today; the future shall not. We must use it now if it is to be of any benefit to mankind.

S O here hath been dawning
    Another blue day;
Think, wilt thou let it
    Slip useless away?

Out of Eternity
    This new day is born;
Into Eternity,
    At night will return.

Behold it aforetime
    No eye ever did;
So soon it for ever
    From all eyes is hid.

116

Here hath been dawning
Another blue day;
Think, wilt thou let it
Slip useless away?

Thomas Carlyle

UNAFRAID

I HAVE no fear. What is in store for me
Shall find me ready for it, undismayed.
God grant my only cowardice may be
    Afraid—to be afraid!

Everard Jack Appleton

BORROWED FEATHERS

Many good, attractive people spoil the merits they have by trying to be
something bigger or showier. It is always best to be one's self.

A ROOSTER one morning was preening his feathers
    That glistened so bright in the sun;
He admired the tints of the various colors
    As he laid them in place one by one.
Now as roosters go he was a fine bird,
    And he should have been satisfied;
But suddenly there as he marched along,
    Some peacock feathers he spied.
They had beautiful spots and their colors were gay—
    He wished that his own could be green;
He dropped his tail, tried to hide it away;
    Was completely ashamed to be seen.

Then his foolish mind hatched up a scheme—
    A peacock yet he could be;
So he hopped behind a bush to undress
    Where the other fowls could not see.

117

He caught his own tail between his bill,
  And pulled every feather out;
And into the holes stuck the peacock plumes;
  Then proudly strutted about.
The other fowls rushed to see the queer sight;
  And the peacocks came when they heard;
They could not agree just what he was,
  But pronounced him a funny bird.

Then the chickens were angry that one of their kind
  Should try to be a peacock;
And the peacocks were mad that one with their tail
  Should belong to a common fowl flock.
So the chickens beset him most cruelly behind,
  And yanked his whole tail out together;
The peacocks attacked him madly before,
  And pulled out each chicken feather.
And when he stood stripped clean down to the skin,
  A horrible thing to the rest,
He learned this sad lesson when it was too late—
  As his own simple self he was best.

Joseph Morris

KEEP ON KEEPIN' ON

The author of these homely stanzas has caught perfectly the spirit which succeeds in the rough-and-tumble of actual life.

IF the day looks kinder gloomy
  And your chances kinder slim,
If the situation's puzzlin'
And the prospect's awful grim,
If perplexities keep pressin'
Till hope is nearly gone,
Just bristle up and grit your teeth
And keep on keepin' on.

Frettin' never wins a fight
And fumin' never pays;
There ain't no use in broodin'
In these pessimistic ways;
Smile just kinder cheerfully
Though hope is nearly gone,
And bristle up and grit your teeth
And keep on keepin' on.

There ain't no use in growlin'
And grumblin' all the time,
When music's ringin' everywhere
And everything's a rhyme.
Just keep on smilin' cheerfully
If hope is nearly gone,
And bristle up and grit your teeth
And keep on keepin' on.

Anonymous

THE DISAPPOINTED

Those who have striven nobly and failed deserve sympathy. Sometimes they also deserve praise unreserved, in that they have refused to do something ignoble that would have led to what the world calls success. They have lived the idea that Macbeth merely proclaimed:

> "I dare do all that may become a man;
> Who dares do more is none."

THERE are songs enough for the hero
   Who dwells on the heights of fame;
I sing of the disappointed—
   For those who have missed their aim.

I sing with a tearful cadence
   For one who stands in the dark,
And knows that his last, best arrow
   Has bounded back from the mark.

I sing for the breathless runner,
    The eager, anxious soul,
Who falls with his strength exhausted,
    Almost in sight of the goal;

For the hearts that break in silence,
    With a sorrow all unknown,
For those who need companions,
    Yet walk their ways alone.

There are songs enough for the lovers
    Who share love's tender pain,
I sing for the one whose passion
    Is given all in vain.

For those whose spirit comrades
    Have missed them on their way,
I sing, with a heart o'erflowing,
    This minor strain today.

And I know the Solar system
    Must somewhere keep in space
A prize for that spent runner
    Who barely lost the race.

For the plan would be imperfect
    Unless it held some sphere
That paid for the toil and talent
    And love that are wasted here.

Ella Wheeler Wilcox

LET ME LIVE OUT MY YEARS

We speak of the comforts and ease of old age, but our noblest selves do not really desire them. We want to do more than exist. We want to be alive to the very last.

L ET me live out my years in heat of blood!
    Let me die drunken with the dreamer's wine!
Let me not see this soul-house built of mud
Go toppling to the dust—a vacant shrine!

Let me go quickly like a candle light
Snuffed out just at the heyday of its glow!
Give me high noon—and let it then be night!
          Thus would I go.

And grant that when I face the grisly Thing,
My song may triumph down the gray Perhaps!
Let me be as a tuneswept fiddlestring
That feels the Master Melody—and snaps.

                              John G. Neihardt

COLUMBUS

This poem pictures courage and high resolution. To the terrors of an unknown sea and the mutinous dismay of the sailors Columbus has but two things to oppose—his faith and his unflinching will. But these suffice, as they always do. In the last four lines of the poem is a lesson for our nation today. The season upon which our ideals have launched us are perilous and uncharted. In some ways our whole voyage of democracy seems futile. Shall we turn back, or shall we, like Columbus, answer the falterers in words that leap like a leaping sword: "Sail on, sail on"?

B EHIND him lay the gray Azores,
    Behind the Gates of Hercules;
Before him not the ghost of shores;
Before him only shoreless seas.
The good mate said: "Now must we pray,
For lo! the very stars are gone.
Brave Adm'r'l speak; what shall I say?"
"Why, say: 'Sail on! sail on! and on!'"

"My men grow mutinous day by day;
My men grow ghastly wan and weak."
The stout mate thought of home; a spray
Of salt wave washed his swarthy cheek.
"What shall I say, brave Adm'r'l, say,
If we sight naught but seas at dawn?"
"Why you shall say at break of day:
'Sail on! sail on! sail on! and on!'"

They sailed and sailed, as winds might blow,
Until at last the blanched mate said:
"Why, now not even God would know
Should I and all my men fall dead.
These very winds forget their way,
For God from these dread seas is gone.
Now speak, brave Adm'r'l; speak and say—"
He said: "Sail on! sail on! and on!"

They sailed. They sailed. Then spake the mate:
"This mad sea shows his teeth tonight.
He curls his lip, he lies in wait,
With lifted teeth, as if to bite!
Brave Adm'r'l, say but one good word:
What shall we do when hope is gone?"
The words leapt like a leaping sword:
"Sail on! sail on! sail on! and on!"

Then, pale and worn, he kept his deck,
And peered through darkness. Ah, that night
Of all dark nights! And then a speck—
A light! A light! A light! A light!
It grew, a starlit flag unfurled!
It grew to be Time's burst of dawn.
He gained a world; he gave that world
Its grandest lesson: "On! sail on!"

Joaquin Miller

122

PER ASPERA

The Latin phrase "per aspera ad astra," is translated sometimes as "through bolts and bars to the stars." It also is the motto of the state of Kansas and translated as "through difficulty to the stars."

THANK God, a man can grow!
    He is not bound
With earthward gaze to creep along the ground:
Though his beginnings be but poor and low,
Thank God, a man can grow!
The fire upon his altars may burn dim,
    The torch he lighted may in darkness fail,
    And nothing to rekindle it avail—
Yet high beyond his dull horizon's rim,
Arcturus and the Pleiads beckon him.

Florence Earle Coates

THE KINGDOM OF MAN

The wisest men know that the greatest world is not outside them. They could, in Shakespeare's phrase, be bounded by a nutshell and count themselves kings of infinite space.

WHAT of the outer drear
    As long as there's inner light;
As long as the sun of cheer
    Shines ardently bright?

As long as the soul's a-wing,
    As long as the heart is true,
What power hath trouble to bring
    A sorrow to you?

No bar can encage the soul,
    Nor capture the spirit free,

As long as old earth shall roll,
    Or hours shall be.

Our world is the world within,
    Our life is the thought we take,
And never an outer sin
    Can mar it or break.

Brood not on the rich man's land,
    Sigh not for the miser's gold,
Holding in reach of your hand
    The treasure untold

That lies in the Mines of Heart,
    That rests in the soul alone—
Bid worry and care depart,
    Come into your own!

John Kendrick Bangs

ABOU BEN ADHEM

"Forgive my enemies?" said the dying man to the priest. "I have none. I've killed them all." This old ideal of exterminating our enemies has by no means disappeared from the earth. But it is waning. "Live and let live" is a more modern slogan, which mounts in turn from mere toleration of other people to a spirit of service and universal brotherhood. Love of our fellow men—has humanity reached any height superior to this?

ABOU BEN ADHEM (may his tribe increase!)
Awoke one night from a deep dream of peace,
And saw, within the moonlight in his room,
Making it rich, and like a lily in bloom,
An angel writing in a book of gold—
Exceeding peace had made Ben Adhem bold,
And to the presence in the room he said,
"What writest thou?"—The vision raised its head,

And with a look made of all sweet accord,
Answered, "The names of those who love the Lord."
"And is mine one?" said Abou. "Nay, not so,"
Replied the angel. Abou spoke more low,
But cheerily still; and said, "I pray thee, then,
Write me as one that loves his fellow-men."

The angel wrote, and vanished. The next night
It came again with a great wakening light,
And showed the names whom love of God had blessed,
And, lo! Ben Adhem's name led all the rest.

Leigh Hunt

THIS WORLD

There is good in life, and there is ill. The question is where we should put the emphasis.

THIS world that we're a-livin' in
    Is mighty hard to beat'
You git a thorn with every rose,
    But *ain't* the roses *sweet!*

Frank L. Stanton

GRAY DAYS

By reckoning up the odds against us and ignoring the forces in our favor, we may indeed close the door of hope. But why not take matters the other way about? Why not see the situation clearly and then throw our own strong purpose in the scales? In the course of a battle an officer reported to Stonewall Jackson that he must fall back because his ammunition had been spoiled by a rainstorm. "So has the enemy's," was the instant reply. "Give them the bayonet." This resolute spirit won the battle.

Hang the gray days!
    The deuce-to-pay days!
The feeling-blue and nothing-to-do days!

The sit-by-yourself-for-there's-nothing-new days!
When the cat that Care killed without excuse
With your inner self's crying, "Oh, what's the use?"
And you wonder whatever is going to become of you,
And you feel that a cipher expresses the sum of you;
And you know that you'll never,
Oh, never, be clever,
Spite of all your endeavor
Or hard work or whatever!
Oh, gee!
What a mix-up you see
When you look at the world where you happen to be!
Where strangers are hateful and friends are a bore,
And you know in your heart you will smile nevermore!
Gee, kid!
Clap on the lid!
It is all a mistake! Give your worries the skid!
There are sunny days coming
    Succeeding the blue
And bees will be humming
    Making honey for you,
And your heart will be singing
    The merriest tune
While April is bringing
    A May and June!
Gray Days?
Play days!
Joy-bringing pay days
And heart-lifting May days!
The sun will be shining in just a wee while
So smile!

Griffith Alexander

LAUGH A LITTLE BIT

"A merry heart doeth good like a medicine"; a little laughter cures many a seeming ill.

HERE'S a motto, just your fit—
Laugh a little bit.
When you think you're trouble hit,
Laugh a little bit.
Look misfortune in the face.
Brave the beldam's rude grimace;
Ten to one 'twill yield its place,
If you have the wit and grit
Just to laugh a little bit.

Keep your face with sunshine lit,
Laugh a little bit.
All the shadows off will flit,
If you have the grit and wit
Just to laugh a little bit.

Cherish this as sacred writ—
Laugh a little bit.
Keep it with you, sample it,
Laugh a little bit. Little ills will sure betide you,
Fortune may not sit beside you,
Men may mock and fame deride you,
But you'll mind them not a whit
If you laugh a little bit.

Edmund Vance Cooke

A SONG OF LIFE

Many of us merely exist and think that we live. What we should regain at all costs is freshness and intensity of being. This need not involve turbulent activity. It may involve quite the opposite.

S AY not, "I live!"
    Unless the morning's trumpet brings
A shock of glory to your soul,
    Unless the ecstasy that sings
Through rushing worlds and insects' wings,
    Sends you upspringing to your goal,
Glad of the need for toil and strife,
    Eager to grapple hands with Life—
Say not, "I live!"

Say not, "I live!"
    Unless the energy that rings
Throughout this universe of fire
    A challenge to your spirit flings,
Here in the world of men and things,
    Thrilling you with a huge desire
To mate your purpose with the stars,
    To shout with Jupiter and Mars—
Say not, "I live!"

Say not, "I live!"
    Such were a libel on the Plan
Blazing within the mind of God
    Ere world or star or sun began.
Say rather, with your fellow man,
    "I grub; I burrow in the sod."
Life is not life that does not flame
    With consciousness of whence it came—
Say not, "I live!"

Angela Morgan

THE TRAINERS

To Benjamin Franklin, seeking recognition and aid for his country at the French court, came news of an American disaster. "Howe has taken Philadelphia," his opponents taunted him. "Oh, no," he answered, "Philadelphia has taken Howe." He shrewdly foresaw that the very magnitude of what the British had done would lull them into overconfidence and inaction and would stir the Americans to more determined effort. Above all, he himself was undisturbed; for to the strong-hearted, trials and reverses are instruments of final success.

MY name is Trouble—I'm a busy bloke—
　　I am the test of Courage—and of Class—
I bind the coward to a bitter yoke,
　　I drive the craven from the crowning pass;
Weaklings I crush before they come to fame;
　　But as the red star guides across the night,
I train the stalwart for a better game;
　　I drive the brave into a harder fight.

My name is Hard Luck—the wrecker of rare dreams—
　　I follow who seek the open fray;
I am the shadow where the far light gleams
　　For those who seek to know the open way;
Quitters I break before they reach the crest,
　　But where the red field echoes with the drums,
I build the fighter for the final test
　　And mold the brave for any drive that comes.

My name is Sorrow—I shall come to all
　　To block the surfeit of an endless joy;
Along the Sable Road I pay my call
　　Before the sweetness of success can cloy;
And weaker souls shall weep amid the throng
　　And fall before me, broken and dismayed;
But braver hearts shall know that I belong
　　And take me in, serene and unafraid.

My name's Defeat—but through the bitter fight,
　　To those who know, I'm something more than friend;
For I can build beyond the wrath of might
　　And drive away all yellow from the blend;

For those who quit, I am the final blow,
   But for the brave who seek their chance to learn,
I show the way, at last, beyond the fore,
   To where the scarlet flames of triumph burn.

Grantland Rice

LIFE

Most of us have failed or gone astray in one fashion or another, at one time or another.   But we need not become despondent at such times.   We should resolve to reap the full benefit of the discovery of our weakness, our folly.

ALL in the dark we grope along,
   And if we go amiss
We learn at least which path is wrong,
   And there is gain in this.

We do not always win the race
   By only running right,
We have to tread the mountain's base
   Before we reach its height.

  •   •   •   •   •   •

But he who loves himself the last
   And knows the use of pain,
Though strewn with errors all his past,
   He surely shall attain.

Some souls there are that needs must taste
   Of wrong, ere choosing right;
We should not call those years a waste
   Which led us to the light.

Ella Wheeler Wilcox

A TOAST TO MERRIMENT

A lady said to Whistler that there were but two painters—himself and Velazquez. He replied: "Madam, why drag in Velazquez?" So it is with Joyousness and Gloom. Both exist—but why drag in Gloom?

MAKE merry! Though the day be gray
Forget the clouds and let's be gay!
How short the days we linger here:
A birth, a breath, and then—the bier!
Make merry, you and I, for when
We part we may not meet again!

What tonic is there in a frown?
You may go up and I go down,
Or I go up and you—who knows
The way that either of us goes?
Make merry! Here's a laugh, for when
We part we may not meet again!

Make merry! What of frets and fears?
There is no happiness in tears.
You tremble at the cloud and lo!
'Tis gone—and so 'tis with our woe,
Full half of it but fancied ills.
Make merry! 'Tis the gloom that kills.

Make merry! There is sunshine yet,
The gloom that promised, let's forget,
The quip and jest are on the wing,
Why sorrow when we ought to sing?
Refill the cup of joy, for then
We part and may not meet again.

A smile, a jest, a joke—alas!
We come, we wonder, and we pass.
  The shadow falls; so long we rest
  In graves, where is no quip or jest.
Good day! Good Cheer! Goodby! For then
We part and may not meet again!

James W. Foley

MISTRESS FATE

"Faint heart never won fair lady." Mistress Fate herself should be courted, not with feminine finesse but with masculine courage and aggression.

FLOUT her power, young man!
  She is merely shrewish, scolding—
She is plastic to your molding,
She is woman in her yielding to the fires desires fan.
  Flout her power, young man!

  Fight her fair, strong man!
Such a serpent love is this—
Bitter wormwood in her kiss!
When she strikes, be nerved and ready;
Keep your gaze both bright and steady,
Chance no rapier-play, but hotly press the quarrel she
    began!
  Fight her fair, strong man!

  Gaze her down, old man!
Now no laughter may defy her,
Not a shaft of scorn come nigh her,
But she waits within the shadows, in dark shadows very
    near.
  And her silence is your fear.
Meet her world-old eyes of warning! Gaze them down

with courage! *Can*
You gaze them down, old man?

William Rose Benét

SLEEP AND THE MONARCH
(From "2 Henry IV.")

The great elemental blessings cannot be "cornered." Indeed they cannot be bought at all but are the natural property of the man whose ways of life are such as to retain them. In this passage, a disappointed and harassed king comments on the slumber that he cannot woo to his couch yet which his humblest subject enjoys.

HOW many thousand of my poorest subjects
Are at this hour asleep! O Sleep! O gentle sleep!
Nature's soft nurse, how have I frighted thee,
That thou no more wilt weigh my eyelids down
And steep my senses in forgetfulness?
Why rather, sleep, liest thou in smoky cribs,
Upon uneasy pallets stretching thee,
And hushed with buzzing night-flies to thy slumber,
Than in the perfumed chambers of the great,
Under the canopies of costly state,
And lulled with sound of sweetest melody?
O thou dull god! why liest thou with the vile
In loathsome beds, and leav'st the kingly couch
A watch-case or a common 'larum bell?
Wilt thou upon the high and giddy mast
Seal up the ship-boy's eyes, and rock his brains
In cradle of the rude imperious surge,
And in the visitation of the winds,
Who take the ruffian billows by the top,
Curling their monstrous heads, and hanging them
With deaf'ning clamor in the slippery clouds,
That with the hurly death itself awakes?
Canst thou, O partial sleep! give thy repose
To the wet sea-boy in an hour so rude,

And in the calmest and most stillest night,
With all appliances and means to boot,
Deny it to a king? Then, happy low, lie down!
Uneasy lies the head that wears a crown.

William Shakespeare

NEVER TROUBLE TROUBLE

To borrow trouble is to contract a debt that any man is better without. If your troubles are not borrowed, they are not likely to be many or great.

I USED to hear a saying
That had a deal of pith;
It gave a cheerful spirit
To face existence with,
Especially when matters
Seemed doomed to go askew.
'Twas *Never trouble trouble*
Till trouble troubles you.

Not woes at hand, those coming
Are hardest to resist;
We hear them stalk like giants,
We see them through a mist.
But big things in the brewing
Are small things in the brew;
So never trouble trouble
Till trouble troubles you.

Just look at things through glasses
That show the evidence;
One lens of them is courage,
The other common sense.
They'll make it clear, misgivings
Are just a bugaboo;
No more you'll trouble trouble
Till trouble troubles you.

St. Clair Adams

CLEAR THE WAY

Humanity is always meeting obstacles. All honor to the men who do not fear obstacles but push them aside and press on. Stephenson was explaining his idea that a locomotive steam engine could run along a track and draw cars after it. "But suppose a cow gets on the track," some one objected. "So much the worse," said Stephenson, "for the cow."

MEN of thought! be up and stirring,
    Night and day;
Sow the seed, withdraw the curtain,
    Clear the way!
Men of action, aid and cheer them,
    As ye may!
There's a fount about to stream,
There's a light about to gleam,
There's a warmth about to glow,
There's a flower about to blow;
There's midnight blackness changing
    Into gray!
Men of thought and men of action,
    Clear the way!

Once the welcome light has broken,
    Who shall say
What the unimagined glories
    Of the day?
What the evil that shall perish
    In its ray?
Aid it, hopes of honest men;
Aid the dawning, tongue and pen;
Aid it, paper, aid it, type,
Aid it, for the hour is ripe;
And our earnest must not slacken
    Into play.
Men of thought and men of action,
    Clear the way!

Lo! a cloud's about to vanish
    From the day;
And a brazen wrong to crumble
    Into clay!
With the Right shall many more
Enter, smiling at the door;
With the giant Wrong shall fall
Many others great and small,
That for ages long have held us
    For their prey.
Men of thought and men of action,
    Clear the way!

Charles Mackay

ONE FIGHT MORE

We need not expect much of the man who, when defeated, gives way either to despair or to a wild impulse for immediate revenge. But from the man who stores up his strength quietly and bides his time for a new effort, we may expect everything.

NOW, think you, Life, I am defeated quite?
    More than a single battle shall be mine
Before I yield the sword and give the sign
    And turn, a crownless outcast, to the night.
Wounded, and yet unconquered in the fight,
    I wait in silence till the day may shine
Once more upon my strength, and all the line
    Of your defenses break before my might.

Mine be that warrior's blood who, stricken sore,
    Lies in his quiet chamber till he hears
Afar the clash and clang of arms, and knows
    The cause he lived for calls for him once more;
And straightway rises, whole and void of fears,
    And arméd, turns him singing to his foes.

Theodosia Garrison

A PSALM OF LIFE

At times this existence of ours seems to be meaningless; whether we have succeeded or whether we have failed appears to make little difference to us, and therefore effort seems scarcely worth while. But Longfellow tells us this view is all wrong. The past can take care of itself, and we need not even worry very much about the future; but if we are true to our own natures, we must be up and doing in the present. Time is short, and mastery in any field of human activity is so long a process that it forbids us to waste our moments. Yet we must learn also how to wait and endure. In short, we must not become slaves to either indifference or impatience but must make it our business to play a man's part in life.

TELL me not, in mournful numbers,
　　Life is but an empty dream!—
For the soul is dead that slumbers,
　　And things are not what they seem.

Life is real! Life is earnest!
　　And the grave is not its goal;
Dust thou art, to dust returnest,
　　Was not spoken of the soul.

Not enjoyment, and not sorrow,
　　Is our destined end or way;
But to act, that each tomorrow
　　Find us farther than today.

Art is long, and Time is fleeting,
　　And our hearts, though stout and brave,
Still, like muffled drums, are beating
　　Funeral marches to the grave.

In the world's broad field of battle,
　　In the bivouac of Life,
Be not like dumb, driven cattle!
　　Be a hero in the strife!

Trust no Future, howe'er pleasant!
   Let the dead Past bury its dead!
Act—act in the living Present!
   Heart within, and God o'erhead!

Lives of great men all remind us
   We can make our lives sublime,
And, departing, leave behind us
   Footprints on the sands of time;

Footprints, that perhaps another,
   Sailing o'er life's solemn main,
A forlorn and shipwrecked brother,
   Seeing, shall take heart again.

Let us, then, be up and doing,
   With a heart for any fate;
Still achieving, still pursuing,
   Learn to labor and to wait.

Henry Wadsworth Longfellow

A CREED

Men may seem sundered from each other; but the soul that each possesses, and the destiny common to all, invest them with a basic brotherhood.

THERE is a destiny that makes us brothers:
   None goes his way alone:
Al that we send into the lives of others
   Comes back into our own.

I care not what his temples or his creeds,
   One thing holds firm and fast—
That into his fateful heap of days and deeds
   The soul of a man is cast.

Edwin Markham

BATTLE CRY

We should win if we can. But in any case we should prove our manhood by fighting.

MORE than half beaten, but fearless,
Facing the storm and the night;
Breathless and reeling but tearless,
Here in the lull of the fight,
I who bow not but before thee,
God of the fighting Clan,
Lifting my fists, I implore Thee,
Give me the heart of a Man!

What though I live with the winners
Or perish with those who fall?
Only the cowards are sinners,
Fighting the fight is all.
Strong is my foe—he advances!
Snapt is my blade, O Lord!
See the proud banners and lances!
Oh, spare me this stub of a sword!

Give me no pity, nor spare me;
Calm not the wrath of my Foe.
See where he beckons to dare me!
Bleeding, half beaten—I go.
Not for the glory of winning,
Not for the feat of the night;
Shunning the battle is sinning—
Oh, spare me the heart to fight!

Red is the mist about me;
Deep is the wound in my side;
"Coward" thou criest to flout me?
O terrible Foe, thou has lied!

Here with my battle before me,
God of the fighting Clan,
That the woman who bore me
Suffered to suckle a Man!

John G. Neihardt

THE HAPPY HEART

One of our objects in life should be to find happiness, contentment. The means of happiness are surprisingly simple. We need not be rich or high-placed or powerful in order to be content. In fact, the lowly are often the best satisfied. Izaak Walton lived the simple life and thanked God that there were so many things in the world of which he had no need.

ART thou poor, yet hast thou golden slumbers?
       O sweet content!
Art thou rich, yet is thy mind perplexed?
       O punishment!
Dost thou laugh to see how fools are vexed
To add to golden numbers, golden numbers?
O sweet content! O sweet, O sweet content!
   Work apace, apace, apace, apace;
   Honest labor bears a lovely face;
Then hey nonny nonny, hey nonny nonny!

Canst drink the waters of the crispéd spring?
       O sweet content!
Swimm'st thou in wealth, yet sink'st in thine own tears?
       O punishment!
Then he that patiently want's burden bears
No burden bears, but is a king, a king!
O sweet content! O sweet, O sweet content!
   Work apace, apace, apace, apace;
   Honest labor bears a lovely face;
Then hey nonny nonny, hey nonny nonny!

Thomas Dekker

IF YOU CAN'T GO OVER OR UNDER, GO AROUND

Often the straight road to the thing we desire is blocked. We should not then weakly give over our purpose but should set about attaining it by some indirect method. A politician knows that one way of getting a man's vote is to please the man's wife, and that one way of pleasing the wife is to kiss her baby.

A BABY mole got to feeling big,
  And wanted to show how he could dig;
So he plowed along in the soft, warm dirt
Till he hit something hard, and it surely hurt!
A dozen stars flew out of his snout;
He sat on his haunches, began to pout;
Then rammed the thing again with his head—
His grandpap picked him up half dead.
"Young man," he said, "though your pate is bone,
You can't butt your way through solid stone.
This bit of advice is good, I've found:
If you can't go over or under, go round."

A traveler came to a stream one day,
And because it presumed to cross his way,
And wouldn't turn round to suit his whim
And change its course to go with him,
His anger rose far more than it should,
And he vowed he'd cross right where he stood.
A man said there was a bridge below,
But not a step would he budge or go.
The current was swift and the bank was steep,
But he jumped right in with a violent leap.
A fisherman dragged him out half-drowned:
"When you can't go over or under, go round."

If you come to a place that you can't get *through*,
Or *over* or *under*, the thing to do
Is to find a way *round* the impassable wall,

Not say you'll go YOUR way or not at all.
You can always get to the place you're going,
If you'll set your sails as the wind is blowing.
If the mountains are high, go round the valley;
If the streets are blocked, go up some alley;
If the parlor-car's filled, don't scorn a freight;
If the front door's closed, go in the side gate.
To reach your goal this advice is sound:
If you can't go over or under, go round!

Joseph Morris

THICK IS THE DARKNESS

How many of us forget when the sun goes down that it will rise again!

THICK is the darkness—
　　Sunward, O, sunward!
Rough is the highway—
　　Onward, still onward!

Dawn harbors surely
　　East of the shadows.
Facing us somewhere
　　Spread the sweet meadows.

Upward and forward!
　　Time will restore us:
Light is above us,
　　Rest is before us.

William Ernest Henley

THE BELLY AND THE MEMBERS
(Adapted from "Coriolanus")

No doubt the world is cursed with grafters and parasites—men who live off the body economic and give nothing substantial in return. But an appearance of

uselessness is not always proof of such. We should not condemn men in igno-
rance. As old as Aesop is the fable of the rebellion of the other members of the
body against the idle unproductiveness of the belly. In this passage, the fable is
used as an answer to the plebeians of Rome who have complained that the patri-
cians are merely an encumbrance.

THERE was a time when all the body's members
    Rebelled against the belly; thus accused it:
That only like a gulf it did remain
I' the midst o' the body, idle and unactive,
Still cupboarding the viand, never bearing
Like labor with the rest, where the other instruments
Did see and hear, devise, instruct, walk, feel,
And, mutually participant, did minister
Unto the appetite and affection common
Of the whole body. Note me this, good friend;
Your most grave belly was deliberate,
Not rash like his accusers, and thus answered:
"True is it, my incorporate friends," quoth he,
"That I receive the general food at first,
Which you do live upon; and fit it is;
Because I am the storehouse and the shop
Of the whole body: but, if you do remember,
I sent it through the rivers of your blood,
Even to the court, the heart, to the seat o' the brain;
And, through the cranks and offices of man,
The strongest nerves and small inferior veins
From me receive that natural competency
Whereby they live. Though all at once cannot
See what I do deliver out to each,
Yet I can make my audit up, that all
From me do back receive the flour of all,
And leave me but the bran." What say you to 't?

William Shakespeare

THE CELESTIAL SURGEON

We may acquire the resolution to be happy by resting on a bed of roses. If that fails us, we should try a bed of nettles.

IF I have faltered more or less
In my great task of happiness;
If I have moved among my race
And shown no glorious morning face;
If beams from happy human eyes
Have moved me not; if morning skies,
Books, and my food, and summer rain
Knocked on my sullen heart in vain—
Lord, thy most pointed pleasure take
And stab my spirit broad awake;
Or, Lord, if too obdurate I,
Choose thou, before that spirit die,
A piercing pain, a killing sin,
And to my dead heart run them in!

Robert Louis Stevenson

MAN, BIRD, AND GOD

Robert Bruce, despairing of his country's cause, was aroused to new hope and purpose by the sight of a spider casting its lines until at last it had one that held. In the following passage, the poet, uncertain as to his own future, yet trusts the providence that guides the birds in their long and uncharted migrations.

I GO to prove my soul!
I see my way as birds their trackless way.
I shall arrive! what time, what circuit first,
I ask not: but unless God send his hail
Or blinding fireballs, sleet or stifling snow,
In some time, his good time, I shall arrive:
He guides me and the bird. In his good time!

Robert Browning

HIS ALLY

The thought of this poem is that man's best helper may be that which gives him no direct aid at all—a sense of humor.

H E fought for his soul, and the stubborn fighting
    Tried hard his strength.
"One needs seven souls for this long requiting."
    He said at length.

"Six times have I come where my first hope jeered me
    And laughed me to scorn;
But now I fear as I never feared me
    To fall forsworn.

"God! when they fight upright at me
    I give them back
Even such blows as theirs that combat me;
    But now, alack!

"They fight with the wiles of fiends escaping
    And underhand.
Six times, O God, and my wounds are gaping!
    I—reel to stand.

"Six battles' span! By this gasping breath
    No pantomime.
'Tis all that I can. I am sick unto death.
    And—a seventh time?

"This is beyond all battles' soreness!"
    Then his wonder cried;
For Laughter, with shield and steely harness,
    Stood up at his side!

William Rose Benét

SUBMISSION

There are times when the right thing to do is to submit. There are times when the right thing to do is to strive, to fight. To put forth one's best effort is itself a reward. But sometimes it brings a material reward also. The frog that after falling into the churn found that it couldn't jump out and wouldn't try was drowned. The frog that kept leaping in brave but seemingly hopeless endeavor at last churned the milk, mounted the butter for a final effort, and escaped.

S UBMISSION? They have preached at that so long.
   As though the head bowed down would right the
     wrong.
   As though the folded hand, the coward heart
Were saintly signs of souls sublimely strong;
   As though the man who acts the waiting part
   And but submits, had little wings a-start.
But may I never reach that anguished plight
Where I at last grow weary of the fight.

Submission: "Wrong of course must ever be
Because it ever was. 'Tis not for me
   To seek a change; to strike the maiden blow.
'Tis best to bow the head and not to see;
   'Tis best to dream, that we need never know
   The truth. To turn our eyes away from woe."
Perhaps. But ah—I pray for keener sight,
And may I not grow weary of the fight.

Miriam Teichner

A PRAYER

Garibaldi, the Italian patriot, said to his men: "I do not promise you ease; I do not promise you comfort. I promise you hardship, weariness, suffering; but I promise you victory."

I DO not pray for peace,
  Nor ask that on my path
The sounds of war shall shrill no more,

The way be clear of wrath.
But this I beg thee, Lord,
    Steel Thou my heart with might,
And in the strife that men call life,
    Grant me the strength to fight.

I do not pray for arms,
    Nor shield to cover me.
What though I stand with empty hand,
    So it be valiantly!
Spare me the coward's fear—
    Questioning wrong or right:
Lord, among these mine enemies,
    Grant me the strength to fight.

I do not pray that Thou
    Keep me from any wound,
Though I fall low from thrust and blow
    Forced fighting to the ground;
But give me wit to hide
    My hurt from all men's sight,
And for my need the while I bleed,
    Lord, grant me strength to fight.

I do not pray that Thou
    Shouldst grant me victory;
Enough to know that from my foe
    I have no will to flee.
Beaten and bruised and banned,
    Flung like a broken sword,
Grant me this thing for conquering—
    Let me die fighting, Lord!

Theodosia Garrison

STABILITY

Whom do we wish for our friends and allies? On whom would we wish to depend in a time of need? Those who are not the slaves of fortune but have made the most of both her buffets and her rewards. Those who control their fears and rash impulses and do not give way to sudden emotion. Amid confusion and disaster men like these will stand, as Jackson did at Bull Run like a veritable stone wall.

S INCE my dear soul was mistress of her choice
        And could of men distinguish, her election
Hath sealed thee for herself; for thou has been
As one, in suffering all, that suffers nothing,
A man that fortune's buffets and rewards
Hast ta'en with equal thanks; and bless'd are those
Whose blood and judgment are so well commingled
That they are not a pipe for fortune's finger
To sound what stop she please. Give me that man
That is not passion's slave, and I will wear him
In my heart's core, ay, in my heart of heart,
As I do thee.

William Shakespeare

THE BARS OF FATE

"There ain't no such beast," ejaculated a farmer as he gazed at the rhinoceros at a circus. His incredulity did not of course do away with the existence of the creature. But our incredulity about many of our difficulties will do away with them. They exist chiefly in our imaginations.

I STOOD before the bars of Fate
    And bowed my head disconsolate;
So high they seemed, so fierce their frown.
I thought no hand could break them down.

Beyond them I could hear the songs
Of valiant men who marched in throngs;
And joyful women, fair and free,
Looked back and waved their hands to me.

I did not cry "Too late! too late!"
Or strive to rise, or rail at Fate,
Or pray to God. My coward heart,
Contented, played its foolish part.

So still I sat, the tireless bee
Sped o'er my head, with scorn for me,
And birds who build their nests in air
Beheld me, as I were not there.

From twig to twig, before my face,
The spiders wove their curious lace,
As they a curtain fine would see
Between the hindering bars and me.

Then, sudden change! I heard the call
Of wind and wave and waterfall;
From heaven above and earth below
A clear command—"ARISE AND GO!"

I upward sprang in all my strength,
And stretched my eager hands at length
To break the bars—no bars were there;
My fingers fell through empty air!

Ellen M. H. Gates

ULTIMATE ACT

It is well to have purposes we can carry out. It also is well to have purposes so
lofty that we cannot carry them out; for these latter are the mighty inner fires
that warm our being at its core and without which our impulse to do even the
lesser things would be feeble.

I HAD rather cut man's purpose deeper than
   Achieving it be crowned as conqueror;
To will divinely is to accomplish more
Than a mere deed: it fills anew the wan

Aspect of life with blood; it draws upon
Sources beyond the common reach and lore
Of mortals, to replenish at its core
The God-impassioned energy of man.
And herewith all the worlds of deed and thought
Quicken again with meaning—pulse and thrill
With Deity—that had forgot His touch.
There is not any act avails so much
As this invisible wedding of the will
With Life—yea, though it seem to accomplish naught.

Henry Bryan Binns

HE WHOM A DREAM HATH POSSESSED

The man possessed by a vison is not perplexed, troubled, restricted, as the rest of us are. He wanders yet is not lost from home, sees a million dawns yet never night descending, faces death and destruction and in them finds triumph.

HE whom a dream hath possessed knoweth no more of
doubting,
For mist and the blowing of winds and the mouthing of
words he scorns;
Not the sinuous speech of schools he hears, but a knightly
shouting,
And never comes darkness down, yet he greeteth a
million morns.

He whom a dream hath possessed knoweth no more of
roaming;
All roads and the flowing of waves the speediest flight
he knows,
But wherever his feet are set, his soul is forever homing,
And going, he comes, and coming he heareth a call and
goes.

He who a dream hath possessed knoweth no more of
sorrow,

At death and the dropping of leaves and the fading of
   suns he smiles,
For a dream remembers no past and scorns the desire of
   a morrow,
And a dream in a sea of doom sets surely the ultimate
   isles.

He whom a dream hath possessed treads the impalpable
   marches,
From the dust of the day's long road he leaps to a
   laughing star,
And the ruin of the worlds that fall he views from eternal
   arches,
And rides God's battlefield in a flashing and golden car.

Sheamus O Sheel

PLAY THE GAME

The Duke of Wellington said that the battle of Waterloo was won on the
cricket fields of Eton. English sport at its best is admirable; it asks outward tri-
umph if possible, but far more it asks that one do his best till the very end and
treat his opponent with courtesy and fairness. The spirit thus instilled at school
has again and again been carried in after life into the large affairs of the nation.

THERE'S a breathless hush in the Close tonight—
   Ten to make and the match to win—
A bumping pitch and a blinding light,
   An hour to play and the last man in.
And it's not for the sake of a ribboned coat
   Or the selfish hope of a season's fame,
But his Captain's hand on his shoulder smote;
   "Play up! Play up! And play the game!"

The sand of the desert is sodden red—
   Red with the wreck of a square that broke;

The Gatling's jammed and the colonel dead,
    And the regiment's blind with dust and smoke.
The river of death has brimmed his banks,
    And England's far and Honor a name,
But the voice of a schoolboy rallies the ranks,
    "Play up! Play up! And play the game!"

This is the word that year by year,
    While in her place the School is set,
Every one of her sons must hear,
    And none that hears it dare forget.
This they all with a joyful mind
    Bear through life like a torch in flame,
And falling, fling to the host behind—
    "Play up! Play up! And play the game!"

Henry Newbolt

THE MAN WHO FRETS AT WORLDLY STRIFE

"Lord, what fools these mortals be!" exclaims Puck in *A Midsummer Night's Dream*. And well might the fairy marvel who sees folk vexing themselves over matters that nine times out of ten come to nothing. Much wiser is the man who smiles at misfortunes, even when they are real ones and affect him personally. Charles Lamb once cheerfully helped to hiss off the stage a play he himself had written.

THE man who frets at worldly strife
    Grows sallow, sour, and thin;
Give us the lad whose happy life
    Is one perpetual grin:

He, Midas-like, turns all to gold—
    He smiles when others sigh,
Enjoys alike the hot and cold,
    And laughs though wet or dry.

There's fun in everything we meet—
    The greatest, worst, and best;
Existence is a merry treat,
    And every speech a jest:

  •   •   •   •   •   •

So, come what may, the man's in luck
    Who turns it all to glee,
And laughing, cries, with honest Puck,
    "Good Lord! what fools ye be."

Joseph Rodman Drake

SERENITY

Calmness of mind to face anything the future may have in store is expressed in this quatrain.

HERE'S a sigh to those who love me
    And a smile to those who hate;
And whatever sky's above me,
    Here's a heart for every fate.

Lord Byron

CLEON AND I

Toward the end of the yacht race in which the America won her historic cup, the English monarch, who was one of the spectators, inquired: "Which boat is first?" "The America seems to be first, your majesty," replied an aide. "And which is second?" asked the monarch. "Your majesty, there seems to be no second." So it is in the race for happiness. The man who is natural, who is open and kind of heart, is always first. The man who is merely rich or sheltered or proud is not even a good second.

CLEON hath a million acres, ne'er a one have I;
    Cleon dwelleth in a palace, in a cottage I;
Cleon hath a dozen fortunes, not a penny I;
Yet the poorer of the twain is Cleon, and not I.

Cleon, true, possesses acres, but the landscape I;
Half the charm to me it yieldeth money can not buy;
Cleon harbors sloth and dullness, freshening vigor I;
He in velvet, I in fustian, richer man am I.

Cleon is a slave to grandeur, free as thought am I;
Cleon fees a score of doctors, need of none have I;
Wealth-surrounded, care-environed, Cleon fears to die;
Death may come, he'll find me ready, happier man am I.

Cleon sees no charm in nature, in a daisy I;
Cleon hears no anthems ringing in the sea and sky;
Nature sings to me forever, earnest listener I;
State for state, with all attendants, who would change?
    Not I.

Charles Mackay

THE PESSIMIST

Most of our ills and troubles are not very serious when we come to examine the realities of them. Or perhaps we expect too much.

NOTHING to do but work,
    Nothing to eat but food,
Nothing to wear but clothes
    To keep from going nude.

Nothing to breathe but air
    Quick as a flash 'tis gone;
Nowhere to fall but off,
    Nowhere to stand but on.

Nothing to comb but hair,
    Nowhere to sleep but in bed,
Nothing to weep but tears,
    Nothing to bury but dead.

Nothing to sing but songs,
  Ah, well, alas! alack!
Nowhere to go but out,
  Nowhere to come but back.

Nothing to see but sights,
  Nothing to quench but thirst,
Nothing to have but what we've got;
  Thus thro' life we are cursed.

Nothing to strike but a gait;
  Everything moves that goes.
Nothing at all but common sense
  Can ever withstand these woes.

Ben King

A PROBLEM TO BE SOLVED

There are irritating, troublesome people about us. Of what use is it to be irritating in our turn or to add to the trouble? Most offenders have their better side. Our wisest course is to find this and upon the basis of it build up a better relationship.

THERE'S a fellow in our office
    Who complains and carps and whines
Till you'd almost do a favor
To his heirs and his assigns.
But I'll tip you to a secret
(And this chap's of course involved)—
He's no foeman to be fought with;
He's a problem to be solved.

  There's a duffer in your district
Whose sheer cussedness is such
He has neither pride nor manners—

155

No, nor gumption, overmuch.
'Twould be great to up and tell him
Where to go. But be resolved—
He's no foeman to be fought with,
Just a problem to be solved.

This old earth's (I'm sometimes thinking)
One menagerie of freaks—
Folks invested with abnormal
Lungs or brains or galls or beaks.
But we're not just shrieking monkeys
In a dim, vast cage revolved;
We're not foemen to be fought with,
Merely problems to be solved.

St. Clair Adams

PROSPICE

Here the poet looks forward to death. He does not ask for an easy death; he does not wish to creep past an experience that all men sooner or later must face, and which many men have faced so heroically. He has fought well in life; he wishes to make the last fight too. The poem was written shortly after the death of Mrs. Browning, and the closing lines refer to her.

FEAR death?—to feel the fog in my throat,
    The mist in my face,
When the snows begin, and the blasts denote
    I am nearing the place,
The power of the night, the press of the storm,
    The post of the foe;
Where he stands, the Arch Fear in a visible form,
    Yet the strong man must go:
For the journey is done and the summit attained,
    And the barriers fall,
Though a battle's to fight ere the guerdon be gained,
    The reward of it all.

I was ever a fighter, so—one fight more,
    The best and the last!
I would hate that death bandaged my eyes and forbore,
    And bade me creep past.
No! let me taste the whole of it, fare like my peers
    The heroes of old,
Bear the brunt, in a minute pay glad life's arrears
    Of pain, darkness and cold.
For sudden the worst turns the best to the brave,
    The black minute's at end,
And the elements' rage, the fiend-voices that rave,
    Shall dwindle, shall blend,
Shall change, shall become first a peace out of pain,
    Then a light, then thy breast,
O thou soul of my soul! I shall clasp thee again,
    And with God be the rest!

Robert Browning

THE GREATNESS OF THE SOUL

Geologists tell us that in the long processes of the ages mountains have been raised and leveled, continents formed and washed away. Astronomers tell us that in space are countless worlds, many of them doubtless inhabited—perhaps by creatures of a lower type than we, perhaps by creatures of a higher. The magnitude of these changes and of these worlds makes the imagination reel. But on one thing we can rely—the greatness of the human soul. On one thing we can confidently build—the men whose spirit is lofty, divine.

FOR tho' the Giant Ages heave the hill
    And break the shore, and evermore
Make and break, and work their will;
Tho' world on world in myriad myriads roll
Round us, each with different powers,
And other forms of life than ours,
What know we greater than the soul?
On God and Godlike men we build our trust.

Alfred Tennyson

HEINELET

What sheer perseverance can accomplish, even in matters of the heart, is revealed in this little poem written in Heine's mood of mingled seriousness and gaiety.

HE asked if she ever could love him.
　　She answered him, no, on the spot.
He asked if she ever could love him.
　　She assured him again she could not.

He asked if she ever could love him.
　　She laughed till his blushes he hid.
He asked if she ever could love him.
　　By God, she admitted she did.

Gamaliel Bradford

STAND FORTH!

As flowers bloom along the edge of the Alpine snow, the human spirit can triumph over difficulties.

STAND forth, my soul, and grip thy woe,
　　Buckle the sword and face thy foe.
What right hast thou to be afraid
When all the universe will aid?
Ten thousand rally to thy name,
Horses and chariots of flame.
Do others fear? Do others fail?
My soul must grapple and prevail.
My soul must scale the mountainside
And with the conquering army ride—
Stand forth, my soul!

Stand forth my soul, and take command.
'Tis I, thy master, bid thee stand.
Claim thou thy ground and thrust thy foe,

Plead not thine enemy should go.
Let others cringe! My soul is free,
No hostile host can conquer me.
There lives no circumstance so great
Can make me yield, or doubt my fate.
My soul must know what kings have known.
Must reach and claim its rightful throne—
Stand forth, my soul!

I ask no truce, I have no qualms,
I seek no quarter and no alms.
Let those who will obey the sod,
My soul sprang from the living God.
'Tis I, the king, who bid thee stand;
Grasp with thy hand my royal hand—
Stand forth!

Angela Morgan

LIONS AND ANTS

ONCE a hunter met a lion near the hungry critter's lair, and the way that lion mauled him was decidedly unfair; but the hunter never whimpered when the surgeons, with their thread, sewed up forty-seven gashes in his mutilated head; and he showed the scars in triumph, and they gave him pleasant fame, and he always blessed the lion that had camped upon his frame. Once that hunter, absent minded, sat upon a hill of ants, and about a million bit him, and you should have seen him dance! And he used up lots of language of a deep magenta tint, and apostrophized the insects in a style unfit to print. And it's thus with worldly troubles; when the big ones come along, we serenely go to meet them, feeling valiant, bold and strong, but the weary little worries with their poisoned stings and smarts, put the lid upon our courage, make us gray, and break our hearts.

Walt Mason

LIFE, NOT DEATH

Sometimes life is so unsatisfying that we think we should like to be rid of it. But we really are not longing for death; we are longing for more life.

WHATEVER crazy sorrow saith,
No life that breathes with human breath
Has ever truly longed for death.

'Tis life, whereof our nerves are scant,
Oh life, not death, for which we pant;
More life, and fuller, that I want.

Alfred Tennyson

THE UNMUSICAL SOLOIST

In any sort of athletic contest a man who individually is good—perhaps even of the very best—may be a poor member of the team because he wishes to do all the playing himself and will not cooperate with his fellows. Every coach knows how such a man hashes the game. The same thing is true in business or in anything else where many people work together; a really capable man often fails because he hogs the center of the stage and wants to be the whole show. To seek petty, immediate triumphs instead of earning and waiting for the big, silent approval of one's own conscience and of those who understand, is a mark of inferiority. It also is a barrier to usefulness, for an egotistical man is necessarily selfish and a selfish man cannot cooperate.

MUSIC hath charms—at least it should;
Even a homely voice sounds good
That sings a cheerful, gladsome song
That shortens the way, however long.
A screechy fife, a bass drum's beat
Is wonderful music to marching feet;
A scratchy fiddle or banjo's thump
May tickle the toes till they want to jump.
But one musician fills the air
With discords that jar folks everywhere.

A pity it is he ever was born—
The discordant fellow who toots his own horn.

He gets in the front where all can see—
"Now turn the spotlight right on me,"
He says, and sings in tones sonorous
His own sweet hallelujah chorus.
Refrain and verse are both the same—
The pronoun I or his own name.
He trumpets his worth with such windy tooting
That louder it sounds than cowboys shooting.
This man's a nuisance wherever he goes,
For the world soon tires of the chap who blows.
Whether mighty in station or hoer of corn,
Unwelcome's the fellow who toots his own horn.

The poorest woodchopper makes the most sound;
A poor cook clatters the most pans around;
The rattling spoke carries least of the load;
And jingling pennies pay little that's owed;
A rooster crows but lays no eggs;
A braggart blows but drives no pegs.
He works out of harmony with any team,
For others are skim milk and he is the cream.
"The world," so far as he can see,
"Consists of a few other folks and ME."
He richly deserves to be held in scorn—
The ridiculous fellow who toots his own horn.

Joseph Morris

ON DOWN THE ROAD

Hazlitt said that the defeat of the Whigs could be read in the shifting and irresolute countenance of Charles James Fox, and the triumph of the Tories in Pitt's "aspiring nose." The empires of the Montezumas are conquered by men who, like Cortez, risk everything in the enterprise and make retreat impossible by burning their ships behind them.

HOLD to the course, though the storms are about you;
Stick to the road where the banner still flies;
Fate and his legions are ready to rout you—
Give 'em both barrels—and aim for their eyes.

Life's not a rose bed, a dream or a bubble,
A living in clover beneath cloudless skies;
And Fate hates a fighter who's looking for trouble,
So give 'im both barrels—and shoot for the eyes.

Fame never comes to the loafers and sitters,
Life's full of knots in a shifting disguise;
Fate only picks on the cowards and quitters,
So give 'em both barrels—and aim for the eyes.

Grantland Rice

PRESS ON

The spirit that has tamed this continent is the spirit that says, "Press on." It appeals, not so much to men in the mass, as to individuals. There is only one way for mankind to go forward. Each individual must be determined that, come what will, he will never quail or recede.

PRESS ON! Surmount the rocky steps,
Climb boldly o'er the torrent's arch;
He fails alone who feebly creeps,
He wins who dares the hero's march.
Be thou a hero! Let thy might
Tramp on eternal snows its way,
And through the ebon walls of night
Hew down a passage unto day.

Press on! If once and twice thy feet
Slip back and stumble, harder try;
From him who never dreads to meet
Danger and death they're sure to fly.

To coward ranks the bullet speeds,
　　While on their breasts who never quail,
Gleams, guardian of chivalric deeds,
　　Bright courage like a coat of mail.

Press on! If Fortune play thee false
　　Today, tomorrow she'll be true;
Who now she sinks she now exalts,
　　Taking old gifts and granting new,
The wisdom of the present hour
　　Makes up the follies past and gone;
To weakness strength succeeds, and power
　　From frailty springs! Press on, press on!

Park Benjamin

MY CREED

　　We all have a philosophy of life, whether or not we formulate it. Does it end in self, or does it include our relations and our duties to our fellows? General William Booth of the Salvation Army was once asked to send a Christmas greeting to his forces throughout the world. His life had been spent in unselfish service; over the cable he sent but one word—OTHERS.

THIS is my creed: To do some good,
　　To bear my ills without complaining,
To press on as a brave man should
　　For honors that are worth the gaining;
To seek no profits where I may,
By winning them, bring grief to others;
To do some service day by day
　　In helping on my toiling brothers.

This is my creed: To close my eyes
　　To little faults of those around me;

To strive to be when each day dies
  Some better than the morning found me;
To ask for no unearned applause,
  To cross no river until I reach it;
To see the merit of the cause
  Before I follow those who preach it.

This is my creed: To try to shun
  The sloughs in which the foolish wallow;
To lead where I may be the one
  Whom weaker men should choose to follow.
To keep my standards always high,
  To find my task and always do it;
This is my creed—I wish that I
  Could learn to shape my action to it.

                              S. E. Kiser

COOPERATION

"We must all hang together, or assuredly we shall all hang separately."
Benjamin Franklin is reported to have said at the signing of the Declaration of
Independence.

IT ain't the guns nor armament,
  Nor funds that they can pay,
But the close cooperation
  That makes them win the day.

It ain't the individual,
  Nor the army as a whole,
But the everlasting teamwork
  Of every bloomin' soul.

                              J. Mason Knox

164

THE NOBLE NATURE

There is a deceptive glamor about mere bigness. Quality may accompany quantity, but it need not. In fact, good things are usually done up in small parcels. "I could eat you at a mouthful," roared a bulky opponent to the small and sickly Alexander H. Stephens. "If you did," replied Stephens quietly, "you'd have more brains in your belly than ever you had in your head."

IT is not growing like a tree
In Bulk, doth make Man better be;
Or standing long an oak, three hundred year,
To fall a log at last, dry, bald, and sere:
A lily of a day
Is fairer far in May,
Although it fall and die that night—
It was the plant and flower of Light.
In small proportions we just beauties see;
And in short measures life may perfect be.

Ben Jonson

DAYS OF CHEER

Thomas Edison said that genius is two parts inspiration, ninety-eight parts perspiration. So happiness is two parts circumstance, ninety-eight parts mental attitude.

"FEELIN' fine," he used to say,
Come a clear or cloudy day,
Wave his hand, an' shed a smile,
Keepin' sunny all th' while.
Never let no bugbears grim
Git a wrastle-holt o' him,
Kep' a-smilin' rain or shine,
Tell you he was "feelin' fine!"

"Feelin' fine," he used to say
Wave his hand an' go his way.

Never had no time to lose,
So he said, fighting blues.
Had a twinkle in his eye
Always when a-goin' by,
Sort o' smile up into mine,
Tell me he was "feelin' fine!"

"Feelin' fine," he'd allus say,
An' th' sunshine seemed to stay
Close by him, or else he shone
With some sunshine of his own.
Didn't seem no clouds could dim
Any happiness for him,
Allus seemed to have a line
Out f'r gladness—"feelin' fine!"

"Feelin' fine," I've heard him say
Half a dozen times a day,
An' as many times I knowed
He was bearin' up a load.
But he never let no grim
Troubles git much holt on him,
Kep' his spirits jest like wine,
Bubblin' up an' "feelin' fine!"

"Feelin' fine"—I hope he'll stay
All his three score that-a-way,
Lettin' his demeanor be
Sech as you could have or me
Ef we tried, an' went along
Spillin' little drops o' song,
Lettin' rosebuds sort o' twine
O'er th' thorns and "feeling fine."

James W. Foley

DE SUNFLOWER AIN'T DE DAISY

"Know yourself," said the Greeks. "Be yourself," bade Marcus Aurelius. "Give yourself," taught the Master. Though the third precept is the noblest, the first and second also are admirable. The second is violated on all hands. Yet to be what nature planned us—to develop our own natural selves—is better than to copy those who are wittier or wiser or otherwise better endowed than we. Genuineness should always be preferred to imitation.

DE sunflower ain't de daisy, and de melon ain't de rose;
   Why is dey all so crazy to be sumfin else dat grows?
Jess stick to de place yo're planted, and do de bes yo knows;
Be de sunflower or de daisy, de melon or de rose.
Don't be what you ain't, jess yo be what you is,
If you am not what you are den yo is not what you is,
If yo're jess a little tadpole, don't yo try try to be de frog;
If you are de tail, don't you try to wag de dawg.
Pass de plate if you can't exhawt and preach;
If yo're jess a little pebble, don't yo try to be de peach;
When a man is what he isn't, den he isn't what he is,
An' as sure as I'm talking, he's a-gwine to get his.

Anonymous

THE DAFFODILS

The poet in lonely mood came suddenly upon a host of daffodils and was thrilled by their joyous beauty. But delightful as the immediate scene was, it was by no means the best part of his experience. For long afterwards, when he least expected it, memory brought back the flowers to the eye of his spirit, filled his solitary moments with thoughts of past happiness, and took him once more (so to speak) into the free open air and the sunshine. Just so for us the memory of happy sights we have seen comes back again to bring us pleasure.

I WANDER'D lonely as a cloud
   That floats on high o'er vales and hills,
When all at once I saw a crowd,
A host of golden daffodils,
Beside the lake, beneath the trees,
Fluttering and dancing in the breeze.

Continuous as the stars that shine
And twinkle on the Milky Way,
They stretch'd in never-ending line
Along the margin of a bay:
Ten thousand saw I at a glance
Tossing their heads in sprightly dance.

The waves beside them danced, but they
Outdid the sparkling waves in glee—
A Poet could not but be gay
In such a jocund company!
I gazed—and gazed—but little thought
What wealth the show to me had brought;

For oft, when on my couch I lie
In vacant or in pensive mood,
They flash upon that inward eye
Which is the bliss of solitude;
And then my heart with pleasure fills,
And dances with the daffodils.

William Wordsworth

A LITTLE THANKFUL SONG

No man is without a reason to be thankful. If he lacks gratitude, the fault
lies with himself.

FOR what are we thankful for? For this:
For the breath and the sunlight of life,
For the love of the child, and the kiss
On the lips of the mother and wife
For roses entwining,
For bud and for bloom,
And hopes that are shining
Like stars in the gloom.

For what are we thankful for? For this:
  The strength and the patience of toil;
For ever the dreams that are bliss—
  The hope of the seed in the soil.
      For souls that are whiter
        From day unto day;
      And lives that are brighter
        From going God's way.

For what are we thankful for? For all:
  The sunlight—the shadow—the song;
The blossoms may wither and fall,
  But the world moves in music along!
      For simple, sweet living,
        ('Tis love that doth teach it)
      A heaven forgiving
        And faith that can reach it!

Frank L. Stanton

TWO RAINDROPS
(A Fable)

TWO little raindrops were born in a shower,
  And one was so pompously proud of his power,
He got in his head an extravagant notion
He'd hustle right off and swallow the ocean.
A blade of grass that grew by the brook
Called for a drink, but no notice he took
Of such trifling things. He must hurry to be
Not a mere raindrop but the whole sea.
A stranded ship needed water to float,
But he could not bother to help a boat.
He leaped in the sea with a puff and a blare—
And nobody even knew he was there!

But the other drop as along it went
Found the work to do for which it was sent:
It refreshed the lily that drooped its head,
And bathed the grass that was almost dead.
It got under the ships and helped them along,
And all the while sang a cheerful song.
It worked every step of the way it went,
Bringing joy to others, to itself content.
At last it came to its journey's end,
And welcomed the sea as an old-time friend.
"An ocean," it said, "there could not be
Except for the millions of drops like me."

Joseph Morris

MY WAGE

We may as well aim high as low, ask much as little. The world will not miss what it gives us, and our reward will largely be governed by our demands.

I BARGAINED with Life for a penny,
And Life would pay no more,
However I begged at evening
When I counted my scanty store;

For Life is a just employer,
He gives you what you ask,
But once you have set the wages,
Why, you must bear the task.

I worked for a menial's hire,
Only to learn, dismayed,
That any wage I had asked of Life,
Life would have paid.

Jessie B. Rittenhouse

THE GIFT

"Trust thyself," says Emerson; "every heart vibrates to that iron string." This is wholesome and inspiring advice, but there is, as always, another side to the question. Many a man falls into absurdities and mistakes because he cannot get outside of himself and look at himself from other people's eyes. We should cultivate the ability to see everything, including ourselves, from more than one standpoint.

O WAD some Pow'r the giftie gie us
　　To see oursels as ithers see us!
It wad frae mony a blunder free us,
　　And foolish notion:
What airs in dress an' gait wad lea'e us,
　　And ev'n devotion!

Robert Burns

PROMETHEUS UNBOUND

In the poem from which this excerpt is taken, Prometheus the Titan has been cruelly tortured for opposing the malignant will of Jupiter. In the end, Prometheus wins a complete outward victory. Better still, by his steadfastness and high purpose he has won a great inward triumph. The spirit that has actuated him and the nature of his achievement are expressed in the following lines.

T O suffer woes which Hope thinks infinite;
　　To forgive wrongs darker than death or night;
　　To defy Power, which seems omnipotent;
To love, and bear; to hope till Hope creates
From its own wreck the thing it contemplates;
　　Neither to change, nor falter, nor repent;
This, like thy glory, Titan, is to be
Good, great and joyous, beautiful and free;
This is alone Life, Joy, Empire, and Victory.

Percy Bysshe Shelly

VICTORY IN DEFEAT

The great, radiant souls of earth—the Davids, the Shakespeares, the Lincolns—know grief and affliction as well as joy and triumph. But adversity is never to them mere adversity; it
> "Doth suffer a sea-change
> Into something rich and strange";

And in the crucible of character their suffering itself is transmuted into song.

D EFEAT may serve as well as victory
   To shake the soul and let the glory out.
When the great oak is straining in the wind,
The boughs drink in new beauty, and the trunk
Sends down a deeper root on the windward side.
Only the soul that knows the mighty grief
Can know the mighty rapture. Sorrows come
To stretch out spaces in the heart for joy.

Edwin Markham

THE RICHER MINES

No man is so poor but that he is a stockholder. Yet many a man has no real riches; his stocks draw dividends in dollars and cents only.

W HEN it comes to buying shares
   In the mines of earth,
May I join the millionaires
   Who are rich in mirth.

Let me have a heavy stake
   In fresh mountain air—
I will promise now to take
   All that you can spare.

When you're setting up your claim
   In the Mines of Glee,
Don't forget to use my name—
   You can count on me.

Nothing better can be won,
    Freer from alloy,
Than a bouncing claim in "Con-
    Solidated Joy."

You can have your Copper Stocks
Gold and tin and coal—
What I'd have within my box
    Has to do with Soul.

John Kendrick Bangs

BRAVE LIFE

To be absolutely without physical fear may not be the highest courage; to shrink and quake, and yet stand at one's post, may be braver still. So of success. It lies less in the attainment of some external end than in holding yourself to your purposes and ideals; for out of high loyalty and effort comes that intangible thing called character, which is no mere symbol of success but success itself.

I DO not know what I shall find on out beyond the final
    fight;
I do not know what I shall meet beyond the last barrage
    of night;
Nor do I care—but this I know—if I but serve within the
    fold
And play the game—I'll be prepared for all the endless
    years may hold.

Life is a training camp at best for what may wait beyond
    the years;
A training camp of toiling days and nights that lean to
    dreams and tears;
But each may come upon the goal and build his soul above
    all Fate
By holding an unbroken faith and taking Courage for a
    mate.

Is not the fight itself enough that man must look to some
behest?
Wherein does Failure miss Success if all engaged but do
their best?
Where does the Victor's cry come in for wreath of fame
or laureled brow
If one he vanquished fought as well as weaker muscle
would allow?

If my opponent in the fray should prove to be a stronger
foe—
Not of his making—but because the Destinies ordained it
so;
If he should win—and I should lose—although I did my
utmost part,
Is my reward the less than his if he should strive with
equal heart?

Brave Life, I hold, is something more than driving
upward to the peak;
Than smashing madly through the strong and crashing
onward through the weak;
I hold the man who makes his fight against the raw game's
crushing odds
Is braver than his brothers are who hold the favor of the
gods.

On by the sky line, faint and vague, in that Far Country
all must know,
No laurel crown of fame may wait beyond the sunset's
glow;
But life has given me the chance to train and serve within
the fold,
To meet the test—and be prepared for all the endless
years may hold.

Grantland Rice

A SONG OF TOMORROW

A night's sleep and a new day—these are excellent things to look forward to when one is weary or in trouble.

L I'L bit er trouble,
    Honey, fer terday;
Yander come Termorrer—
    Shine it all away!

Rainy Sky is sayin',
    "Dis'll never do!
Fetch dem rainbow ribbons,
    En I'll dress in blue!"

Frank L. Stanton

THE GLAD SONG

Gladness begins with the first person, with you. But it may spread far, like the ripples when you toss a stone in the water.

S ING a song, sing a song,
    Ring the glad-bells all along;
Smile at him who frowns at you,
He will smile and then they're two.

Laugh a bit, laugh a bit,
Folks will soon be catching it,
Can't resist a happy face;
World will be a merry place.

Laugh a Bit and Sing a Song,
Where they are there's nothing wrong;
Joy will dance the whole world through,
But it must begin with you.

Joseph Morris

PAINTING THE LILY

Many people are not content to let well enough alone but spoil what they have by striving for an unnecessary and foolish improvement. If they have a rich title, they try to ornament it still further; if they have refined gold, they try to gild it; if they have a lily, they try to paint it into still purer color.

THEREFORE, to be possessed with double pomp,
    To guard a title that was rich before,
To gild refinéd gold, to paint the lily,
To throw a perfume on the violet,
Unto the rainbow, or with taper-light
To see the beauteous eye of heaven to garnish,
Is wasteful and ridiculous excess.

William Shakespeare

A PRETTY GOOD WORLD

The world has its faults, but few of us would give it up till we have to.

PRETTY good world if you take it all round—
    Pretty good world, good people!
Better be on than under the ground—
    Pretty good world, good people!
Better be here where the skies are as blue
As the eyes of your sweetheart a-smilin' at you—
Better than lyin' 'neath daisies and dew—
    Pretty good world, good people!

Pretty good world with its hopes and its fears—
    Pretty good world, good people!
Sun twinkles bright through the rain of its tears—
    Pretty good world, good people!
Better be here, in the pathway you know—
Where the thorn's in the garden where sweet roses grow,
Than to rest where you feel not the fall o' the snow—
    Pretty good world, good people!

Pretty good world! Let us sing it that way—
    Pretty good world, good people!
Make up your mind that you're in it to stay—
    At least for a season, good people!
Pretty good world, with its dark and its bright—
Pretty good world, with its love and its light;
Sing it that way till you whisper, "Goodnight!"—
    Pretty good world, good people!

Frank L. Stanton

ODE TO DUTY

In the first stanza, the poet hails duty as coming from God. It is a light to guide us and a rod to check. To obey it does not lead to victory; to obey it is victory—is to live by a high, noble law. In the second stanza, he admits that some people do right without driving themselves to it—do it by instinct and "the genial sense of youth." In stanza 3, he looks forward to a time when all people will be thus blessed, but he thinks that as yet it is unsafe for most of us to lose touch completely with stern, commanding duty. In stanzas 4 and 5, he states that he himself has been too impatient of control, has wearied himself by changing from one desire to another, and now wishes to regulate his life by some great abiding principle. In stanza 6, he declares that duty, though stern, is benignant; the flowers bloom in obedience to it, and the stars keep their places. In the final stanza, he dedicates his life to its service.

S TERN Daughter of the Voice of God!
    O Duty! if that name thou love
Who art a light to guide, a rod
To check the erring, and reprove;
Thou who art victory and law
When empty terrors overawe;
From vain temptations dost set free,
And calm'st the weary strife of frail humanity!

There are who ask not if thine eye
Be on them; who, in love and truth
Where no misgiving is, rely
Upon the genial sense of youth:
Glad hearts! without reproach or blot,

177

Who do thy work, and know it not:
　Oh! if through confidence misplaced
They fail, thy saving arms, dread Power! around them cast.

Serene will be our days and bright
And happy will our nature be
When love is an unerring light,
And joy its own security.
And they a blissful course may hold
Ev'n now, who, not unwisely bold,
　Live in the spirit of this creed;
Yet seek thy firm support, according to their need.

I, loving freedom, and untried,
No sport of every random gust,
Yet being to myself a guide,
Too blindly have reposed my trust:
And oft, when in my heart was heard
Thy timely mandate, I deferr'd
The task, in smoother walks to stray;
But thee I know would serve more strictly, if I may.

Through no disturbance of my soul
Or strong compunction in me wrought,
I supplicate for thy control,
But in the quietness of thought:
Me this uncharter'd freedom tires;
I feel the weight of chance-desires;
My hopes no more must change their name;
I long for a repose that ever is the same.

Stern Lawgiver! yet thou dost wear
The Godhead's most benignant grace,
Nor know we anything so fair
As is the smile upon thy face;
Flowers laugh before thee on their beds,
And fragrance in thy footing treads;

Thou dost preserve the Stars from wrong;
And the most ancient Heavens, through Thee, are fresh and
strong.

To humbler functions, awful Power!
I call thee: I myself commend
Unto thy guidance from this hour;
Oh let my weakness have an end!
Give unto me, made lowly wise,
The spirit of self-sacrifice;
The confidence of reason give;
And in the light of truth thy Bondman let me live.

William Wordsworth

THE SYNDICATED SMILE

A ready and sincere friendliness is the one thing we can show to every human being, whether we know him or not. The world is full of perplexed and lonely people whom even a smile or a kind look will help. Yet that which is so easy to give we too often reserve for a few, and those perhaps the least appreciative.

I KNEW a girl who had a beau
And his name wasn't Adams—
No child of hers would ever call
The present writer "daddums."
I didn't love the girl, but still
I found her most beguiling;
And so did all the other chaps—
She did it with her smiling.
"I'm not a one-man girl," she said—
"Of smiles my beau first took his;
But some are left; I'll syndicate
And pass them round like cookies."

That syndicated smile!
When trouble seemed the most in style,

                    It heartened us—
                        That indicated,
                            Syndicated
                                Smile.

        It's not enough to please your boss
    Or fawn round folks with bankrolls;
    Be just as friendly to the guys
    Whose homespun round their shank rolls.
    The best investment in the world
    Is goodwill, twenty carat;
    It costs you nothing, brings returns;
    So get yours out and air it.
    A niggard of good nature cheats
    Himself and wrongs his fellows.
    You'd serve mankind? Then be less close
    With friendly nods and hellos.

                    The syndicated smile!
                If you have kept it all the while,
                You've vindicated
                    The indicated,
                        Syndicated
                            Smile.

                                    St. Clair Adams

FAIRY SONG

The great beneficent forces of life are not exhausted when once used but are recurrent. The sun rises afresh each new day. Once a year the springtime returns, and "God renews His ancient rapture." So it is with our joys. They do not stay by us constantly; they pass from us and are gone; but we need not trouble ourselves—they are sure to come back.

S HED no tear! O shed no tear!
    The flower will bloom another year.

Weep no more! O weep no more!
Young buds sleep in the root's white core.
Dry your eyes! O dry your eyes,
For I was taught in Paradise
To ease my breast of melodies—
                    Shed no tear.

Overhead! Look overhead,
'Mong the blossoms white and red—
Look up, look up—I flutter now
On this flush pomegranate bough.
See me! 'tis this silvery bill
Ever cures the good man's ill.
Shed no tear! O shed no tear!
The flowers will bloom another year.
Adieu, adieu—I fly, adieu,
I vanish in the heaven's blue—
                    Adieu, adieu!

John Keats

PRAISE THE GENEROUS GODS FOR GIVING

Some of us find joy in toil, some in art, some in the open air and the sunshine. All of us find it in simply being alive. Life is the gift no creature in his right mind would part with. As Milton asks,
> "For who would lose,
> Though full of pain, this intellectual being,
> To perish rather, swallowed up and lost
> In the wide womb of uncreated night,
> Devoid of sense and motion?"

PRAISE the generous gods for giving
    In a world of wrath and strife,
With a little time for living,
    Unto all the joy of life.

At whatever source we drink it,
    Art or love or faith or wine,

In whatever terms we think it,
It is common and divine.

Praise the high gods, for in giving
This to man, and this alone,
They have made his chance of living
Shine the equal of their own.

William Ernest Henley

COWARDS

We might as well accept the inevitable as the inevitable. There is no escaping death and taxes.

COWARDS die many times before their deaths:
The valiant never taste of death but once.
Of all the wonders that I yet have heard,
It seems to me most strange that men should fear;
Seeing that death, a necessary end,
Will come, when it will come.

William Shakespeare

THE WORD

The Cumaean sibyl offered Tarquin the Proud nine books for what seemed an exorbitant sum. He refused. She burned three of the books and placed the same price on the six as on the original nine. Again he refused. She burned three more books, and offered the remainder for the sum she first named. This time Tarquin accepted. The books were found to contain prophecies and invaluable directions regarding Roman policy, but, alas, they were no longer complete. So it is with joy. To take it now is to get it in its entirety. To defer until some other occasion is to get less of it—at the same cost.

TODAY, whatever may annoy,
The word for it is Joy, just simple joy:

The joy of life;
The joy of children and of wife;
The joy of bright blue skies;
The joy of rain; the glad surprise
Of twinkling stars that shine at night;
The joy of winged things upon their flight;
The joy of noonday, and the tried,
True joyousness of eventide;
The joy of labor and of mirth;
The joy of air, and sea, and earth—
The countless joys that ever flow from Him
Whose vast beneficence doth dim
The lustrous light of day,
And lavish gifts divine upon our way.
Whate'er there be of Sorrow
I'll put off till Tomorrow,
And when Tomorrow comes, why, then
'Twill be Today, and Joy again!

John Kendrick Bangs

ENVOI

Franklin K. Lane stipulated that when he died his body should be cremated and the ashes scattered from El Capitan over the beautiful Yosemite Valley. He thus symbolized what many of us feel—the unity of our deeper and finer selves with the eternal life and loveliness of nature.

OH seek me not within a tomb;
　　Thou shalt not find me in the clay!
I pierce a little wall of gloom
To mingle with the Day!

I brothered with the things that pass,
Poor giddy Joy and puckered Grief;
I go to brother with the Grass
And with the sunning Leaf.

Not Death can sheathe me in a shroud;
A joy-sword whetted keen with pain,
I join the armies of the Cloud
The Lightning and the Rain.

Oh subtle in the sap athrill,
Athletic in the glad uplift,
A portion of the Cosmic Will,
I pierce the planet-drift.

My God and I shall interknit
As rain and Ocean, breath and Air;
And oh, the luring thought of it
Is prayer!

John G. Neihardt

JAW

We all like a firm, straightforward chin provided it is not ruled by a wagging, gossiping tongue.

THIS fellow's jaw is built so frail
   That you could break it like a weed;
That fellow's chin retreats until
You'd think it in a wild stampede.
Defects like these but show how soon
The purpose droops, the spirits flag—
We like a jaw that's made of steel,
Just so it's not inclined to wag.

The lower jaw should be as strong
And changeless as a granite cliff;
Its very look should be a *thus*
And not a *maybe, somehow, if*;
Should mark a soul so resolute

It will not fear or cease or lag—
We need a rugged mandible,
Provided we don't let it wag.

Yes, with endurance, let it too
A tender modesty possess;
And to its grim strength let it add
The gracious power of gentleness.
Above all, let its might of deeds
Induce no loud or vulgar brag—
We like to see a good, firm jaw,
But do no wish to hear it wag.

St. Clair Adams

THE CONQUEROR

Age is wise; it attempts nothing impossible. Youth is wiser; it believes nothing impossible. Age conserves more; youth accomplishes more. Between the two is an irreconcilable difference.

"Crabbéd age and youth
Cannot live together,"

as Shakespeare says. And the sympathy of the world is with youth. It is better so; for though many cherished things would be saved from sacrifice if rash immaturity were more often checked, progress would be stayed if life were dominated by sterile and repressive age.

ROOM for me, graybeards, room, make room!
Menace me not with your eyes of gloom;
For my arms are strong and your own are weak,
And if my plea to you be denied
I'll thrust your wearying forms aside.
Pity you? Yes, but I cannot stay;
I am the spirit of Youth; make way!

Room for me, timid ones, room, make room!
Little I care for your fret and fume—
I dare whatever is mine to meet,

I laugh at sorrow and jeer defeat;
To doubt and doubters I give the lie,
And fear is stilled as I swagger by,
And life's a fight and I seek the fray;
I am the spirit of Youth; make way!

Room for me, mighty ones, room, make room!
I fear no power and dread no doom;
And you who curse me and you who bless
Alike must bow to my dauntlessness.
I topple the king from his golden throne,
I smash old idols of brass and stone,
I am not hampered by yesterday.
Room for the spirit of Youth; make way!

Room for me, all of you, make me room!
Where the rifles clash and the cannon boom,
Where glory beckons or love or fame
I plunge me heedlessly in the game.
The old, the wary, the wise, the great,
They cannot stay me, for I am Fate,
The brave young master of all good play,
I am the spirit of Youth; make way!

Berton Braley

IS IT RAINING, LITTLE FLOWER?

"Sweet are the uses of adversity." They bring us benefits not otherwise to be had. To mope because of them is foolish. Showers alternate with sunshine, sorrows with pleasure, pain and weariness with comfort and rest; but accept the one as necessary to the other, and you will enjoy both.

IS it raining, little flower?
   Be glad of rain.
Too much sun would wither thee,
   'Twill shine again.
The sky is very black, 'tis true,

But just behind it shines
    The blue.

Art thou weary, tender heart?
    Be glad of pain;
In sorrow the sweetest things will grow
    As flowers in the rain.
God watches and thou wilt have sun
    When clouds their perfect work
        Have done.

Anonymous

GRADATIM

In the old fable, the tortoise won the race from the hare, not by a single burst of speed but by plodding on steadily, tirelessly. In the Civil War, it was found that Lee's army could not be overwhelmed in a single battle, but one Federal general perceived that it could be worn down by time and the pressure of numbers. "I propose," said Grant, "to fight it out on this line if it takes all summer." It took more than a summer; it took nearly a year—but he did it. In the moral realm likewise, "All things excellent are as difficult as they are rare." Character is not attained overnight. The only way to develop moral muscles is to exercise them patiently and long.

HEAVEN is not reached at a single bound;
    But we build the ladder by which we rise
    From the lowly earth to the vaulted skies,
And we mount to its summit, round by round.

I count this thing to be grandly true:
    That a noble deed is a step towards God—
    Lifting the soul from the common clod
To a purer air and a broader view.

We rise by the things that are under feet;
    By what we have mastered of food and gain;
    By the pride deposed and the passion slain,
And the vanquished ills that we hourly meet.

We hope, we aspire, we resolve, we trust,
    When the morning calls us to life and light,
    But our hearts grow weary, and, ere the night,
Our lives are trailing the sordid dust.

We hope, we resolve, we aspire, we pray,
    And we think that we mount the air on wings
    Beyond the recall of sensual things,
While our feet still cling to the heavy clay.

Wings for the angels, but feet for men!
    We may borrow the wings to find the way—
    We may hope, and resolve, and aspire, and pray;
But our feet must rise, or we fall again.

Only in dreams is a ladder thrown
    From the weary earth to the sapphire walls;
    But the dreams depart, and the vision falls,
And the sleeper wakes on his pillow of stone.

Heaven is not reached at a single bound;
    But we build the ladder by which we rise
    From the lowly earth to the vaulted skies,
And we mount to its summit, round by round.

J. G. Holland

RULES FOR THE ROAD

Ardor of sinew and spirit—what else do we need to make our journey prosperous and happy?

STAND straight:
    Step firmly, throw your weight:
The heaven is high above your head,
The good gray road is faithful to your tread.

Be strong:
Sing to your heart a battle song:
Though hidden foemen lie in wait,
Something is in you that can smile at Fate.

Press through:
Nothing can harm if you are true.
And when the night comes, rest:
The earth is friendly as a mother's breast.

Edwin Markham

LIFE

"What is life?" we ask. "Just one darned thing after another," the cynic replies. Yes, a multiplicity of forces and interests, and each of them, even the disagreeable, may be of real help to us. It's good for a dog, says a shrewd philosopher, to be pestered with fleas; it keeps him from thinking too much about being a dog.

WHAT'S life? A story or a song;
    A race on any track;
A gay adventure, short or long,
    A puzzling nut to crack;
A grinding task; a pleasant stroll;
    A climb; a slide down hill;
A constant striving for a goal;
    A cake; a bitter pill;
A pit where fortune flouts or stings;
    A playground full of fun—
With many any of these things;
    With others all in one.
What's life? To love the things we see;
    The hills that touch the skies;
The smiling sea; the laughing lea;
    The light in woman's eyes;
To work and love the work we do;

To play a game that's square;
To grin a bit when feeling blue;
    With friends our joys to share;
To smile, though games be lost or won;
    To earn our daily bread—
And when at last the day is done
    To tumble into bed.

Griffith Alexander

BORROWING TROUBLE

It is bad enought to cry over spilt milk. But many of us do worse; we cry over milk that we think is going to be spilt. In line 1, sic=such; 2, a'=all; 3, nae=no; 4, enow=enough; 5, hae=have; sturt=fret, trouble.

BUT human bodies are sic fools,
    For a' their colleges an' schools,
That when nae real ills perplex them,
They mak enow themsels to vex them;
An' ay the less they hae to sturt them,
In like proportion less will hurt them.

Robert Burns

UNDISMAYED

A convict explained to a visitor why he had been sent to the penitentiary. "They can't put you in here for that!" the visitor exclaimed. "They did," replied the convict. So smiling seems a futile thing. Apparently it cannot get us any-where—but it does.

HE came up smilin'—used to say
    He made his fortune that-a-way;
He had hard luck a-plenty, too,
But settled down an' fought her through;
An' every time he got a jolt
He jist took on a tighter holt,
Slipped back some when he tried to climb
But came up smilin' every time.

190

He came up smilin'—used to git
His share o' knocks, but he had grit,
An' if they hurt he didn't set
Around th' grocery store an' fret.
He jist grabbed Fortune by th' hair
An' hung on till he got his share.
He had th' grit in him to stay
An' come up smilin' every day.

He jist gripped hard an' all alone
Like a set bull-pup with a bone,
An' if he got shook loose, why then
He got up an' grabbed holt again.
He didn't have no time, he'd say,
To bother about yesterday,
An' when there was a prize to win
He came up smilin' an' pitched in.

He came up smilin'—good fer him!
He had th' grit an' pluck an' vim,
So he's on Easy Street, an' durned
If I don't think his luck is earned!
No matter if he lost sometimes,
He's got th' stuff in him that climbs,
An' when his chance was mightly slim,
He came up smilin'—good fer him!

James W. Foley

A HERO

If defeat strengthens and sweetens character, it is not defeat at all but victory.

HE sang of joy; whate'er he knew of sadness
He kept for his own heart's peculiar share:
So well he sang, the world imagined gladness
To be sole tenant there.

For dreams were his, and in the dawn's fair shining,
    His spirit soared beyond the mounting lark;
But from his lips no accent of repining
    Fell when the days grew dark;

And though contending long dread Fate to master,
    He failed at last her enmity to cheat,
He turned with such a smile to face disaster
    That he sublimed defeat.

Florence Earle Coates

WILL

"I can resist anything but temptation," says a character in one of Oscar Wilde's plays. Too many of us have exactly this strength of will. We perhaps do not fall into gross crime, but because of our flabby resolution our lives become purposeless, negative, negligible. No one would miss us in particular if we were out of the way.

I

O WELL for him whose will is strong!
    He suffers, but he will not suffer long;
For him nor moves the loud world's random mock,
Nor all Calamity's hugest waves confound,
Who seems a promontory of rock,
That, compass'd round with turbulent sound,
In middle ocean meets the surging shock,
Tempest-buffeted, citadel-crown'd.

II

But ill for him who, bettering not with time,
Corrupts the strength of heaven-descended Will,
And ever weaker grows thro' acted crime,
Or seeming-genial venial fault,
Recurring and suggesting still!

He seems as one whose footsteps halt,
Toiling in immeasurable sand,
And o'er a weary sultry land,
Far beneath a blazing vault,
Sown in a wrinkle of the monstrous hill,
The city sparkles like a grain of salt.

Alfred Tennyson

FABLE

To be impressed by a thing merely because it is big is a human failing. Yet our standard of judgment would be truer if we considered, instead, the success of that thing in performing its own particular task. And quality is better than quantity. The lioness in the old fable was being taunted because she bore only one offspring at a time, not a numerous litter. "It is true," she admitted, "but that one is a lion."

THE mountain and the squirrel
Had a quarrel,
And the former called the latter "Little Prig";
Bun replied,
"You are doubtless very big;
But all sorts of things and weather
Must be taken in together,
To make up a year
And a sphere.
And I think it no disgrace
To occupy my place.
If I'm not so large as you,
You are not so small as I,
And not half so spry.
I'll not deny you make
A very pretty squirrel track;
Talents differ; all is well and wisely put;
If I cannot carry forests on my back,
Neither can you crack a nut."

Ralph Waldo Emerson

DUTY

WHEN Duty comes a-knocking at your gate,
Welcome him in, for if you bid him wait,
He will depart only to come once more
And bring seven other duties to your door.

Edwin Markham

PRAYER FOR PAIN

"The thief steals from himself. The swindler swindles himself," says Emerson. Apparent gain may be actual loss; material escape may be spiritual imprisonment. Any one may idle; but the men who are not content unless they climb the unscalable mountains or cross the uncharted seas or bear the burdens that others shrink from, are the ones who keep the heritage of the spirit undiminished.

I DO not pray for peace nor ease,
Nor truce from sorrow:
No supplicant on servile knees
Begs here against tomorrow!

Lean flame against lean flame we flash,
O, Fates that meet me fair;
Blue steel against blue steel we clash—
Lay on, and I shall dare!

But Thou of deeps the awful Deep,
Thou Breather in the clay,
Grant this my only prayer—Oh keep
My soul from turning gray!

For until now, whatever wrought
Against my sweet desires,
My days were smitten harps strung taut,
My nights were slumbrous lyres.

And howsoe'er the hard blow rang
Upon my battered shield,

Some lark-like, soaring spirit sang
Above my battlefield.

And through my soul of stormy night
The zigzag blue flame ran.
I asked no odds—I fought my fight—
Events against a man.

But no—at last—the gray mist chokes
And numbs me. *Leave me pain!*
Oh let me feel the biting strokes
That I may fight again!

John G. Neihardt

STEADFAST

No one ever has a trouble so great that some other person has not a greater. The thought of the heroism shown by those more grievously afflicted than we helps us to bear our own ills patiently.

I F I can help another bear an ill
By bearing mine with somewhat of good grace—
Can take Fate's thrusts with not too long a face
And help him through his trials, then I WILL!
For do not braver men than I decline
To bow to troubles graver, far, than mine?

Pain twists this body? Yes, but it shall not
Distort my soul, by all the gods that be!
And when it's done its worst, Pain's victory
Shall be an empty one! Whate'er my lot,
My banner, ragged, but nailed to the mast,
Shall fly triumphant to the very last!

Others so much worse off than I have fought;
Have smiled—have met defeat with unbent head

They shame me into following where they led.
Can I ignore the lesson they have taught?
Strike hands with me! Dark is the way we go,
But souls-courageous line it—that I know!

Everard Jack Appleton

IF

If I were fire I'd burn the world away
If I were wind I'd turn my storms thereon.
If I were water I'd soon let it drown.

Cecco Angolieri

IF I were fire I'd seek the frozen North
And warm it till it blossomed fairly forth
And in the sweetness of its smiling mien
Resembled some soft southern garden scene.
And when the winter came again I'd seek
The chilling homes of lowly ones and meek
And do my small but most efficient part
To bring a wealth of comfort to the heart.

If I were wind I'd turn my breath upon
The calm-bound mariner until, anon,
The eager craft on which he sailed should find
The harbor blest towards which it hath inclined.
And in the city streets, when summer's days
Were withering the souls with scorching rays,
I'd seek the fevered brow and aching eyes
And take to them a touch of Paradise.

If I were water it would be my whim
To seek out all earth's desert places grim,
And turn each arid acre to a fair
Lush home of flowers and oasis rare.
Resolved in dew, I'd nestle in the rose.

As summer rain I'd ease the harvest woes,
And where a tear to pain would be relief,
A tear I'd be to kill the sting of grief.

If I were gold, I'd seek the poor man's purse.
I'd try to win my way into the verse
Of some grand singer of Man's Brotherhood,
And prove myself so pure, so fraught with good,
That all the world would bless me for the cup
Of happiness I'd brought for all to sup.
And when at last my work of joy was o'er
I'd be content to die, and be no more!

John Kendrick Bangs

A PHILOSOPHER

"The web or our life is of mingled yarn, good and ill together," says Shakespeare. It behooves us therefore to find the good and to make the best of the ill. Two men were falling from an airplane. "I'll bet you five dollars," said one, "that I hit the ground first."

To take things as they be—
    Thet's my philosophy.
No use to holler, mope, or cuss—
If they was changed they might be wuss.

If rain is pourin' down,
    An' lightnin' buzzin' roun',
I ain't a-fearin' we'll be hit,
But grin thet I ain't out in it.

If I got deep in debt—
    It hasn't happened yet—
And owed a man two dollars, Gee!
Why I'd be glad it wasn't three.

If some one come along,
And tried to do me wrong,
Why I should sort of take a whim
To thank the Lord I wasn't him.

I never seen a night
So dark there wasn't light
Somewheres about if I took care
To strike a match and find out where.

John Kendrick Bangs

THE LIFE WITHOUT PASSION

A person may feel deeply without shouting his emotion to the skies or be strong without seizing occasions to exhibit his strength. In truth, we distrust the power that makes too much a display of itself. Let it exert itself only to the point of securing the ends that are really necessary. Restraint, self-control are more mighty than might unshackled, just as a self-possessed opponent is more dangerous than a frenzied one. A good quality, if abused or allowed free sway, becomes a force for evil and does its owner more harm than if he had not possessed it in the first place.

THEY that have power to hurt, and will do
   none,
That do not do the thing they most do show,
Who, moving others, are themselves as stone,
Unmovéd, cold, and to temptation slow—

They rightly do inherit heaven's graces,
And husband nature's riches from expense;
They are the lords and owners of their faces,
Others, but stewards of their excellence.

The summer's flower is to the summer sweet,
Though to itself it only live and die;
But if that flower with base infection meet,
The basest weed outbraves his dignity:

For sweetest things turn sourest by their deeds;
Lilies that fester smell worse than weeds.

William Shakespeare

CHARACTER OF A HAPPY LIFE

"I'd rather be right than President," said Henry Clay. It is to men who are animated by this spirit that the greatest satisfaction in life comes. For true blessedness does not lie far off and above us. It is close at hand. Booker T. Washington once told a story of a ship that had exhausted its supply of fresh water and signaled its need to a passing vessel. The reply was, "Send down your buckets where you are." Thinking there was some misunderstanding, the captain repeated his signal, only to be answered as before. This time he did as he was bidden and secured an abundance of fresh water. His ship was opposite the mouth of a mighty river that still kept its current unmingled with the waters of the ocean.

HOW happy is he born and taught
    That serveth not another's will;
Whose armor is his honest thought
    And simple truth his utmost skill!

Whose passions not his masters are,
    Whose soul is still prepared for death,
Not tied unto the world with care
    Of public fame or private breath;

Who envies none that chance doth raise
    Or vice; who never understood
How deepest wounds are given by praise
    Nor rules of state, but rules of good;

Who hath his life from rumors freed,
    Whose conscience is his strong retreat;
Whose state can neither flatterers feed,
    Nor ruin make accusers great;

Who God doth late and early pray
　　More of his grace than gifts to lend;
And entertains the harmless day
　　With a well-chosen book or friend;

—This man is freed from servile bands
　　Of hope to rise or fear to fall;
Lord of himself, though not of lands;
　　And having nothing, yet hath all.

Sir Henry Wotton

ESSENTIALS

The things here named are essential to a happy and successful life. They
may not be the only essentials.

R OLL up your sleeves, lad, and begin;
　　Disarm misfortune with a grin;
Let discontent not wag your chin—
Let gratitude.

　　Don't try to find things all askew;
Don't be afraid of what is new
Nor banish as unsound, untrue,
A platitude.

　　If folks don't act as you would choose,
Remember life is varied; use
Your common sense; don't get the blues;
Show latitude.

　　Sing though in quavering sharps and flats,
Love though the folk you love are cats,
Work though you're worn and weary—that's
The attitude.

St. Clair Adams

THE STONE REJECTED

The story here poetically retold of the great Florentine sculptor shows how much a lofty spirit may make of unpromising material.

FOR years it had been trampled in the street
    Of Florence by the drift of heedless feet—
The stone that star-touched Michael Angelo
Turned to that marble loveliness we know.

You mind the tale—how he was passing by
When the rude marble caught his Jovian eye,
That stone men had dishonored and had thrust
Out to the insult of the wayside dust.
He stooped to lift it from its mean estate,
And bore it on his shoulder to the gate,
Where all day long a hundred hammers rang.
And soon his chisel round the marble sang,
And suddenly the hidden angel shone:
It had been waiting prisoned in the stone.

Thus came the cherub with the laughing face
That long has lighted up an altar-place.

Edwin Markham

GOOD DEEDS

The influence of good deeds usually extends far beyond the limits we can see or trace; but as well not have the power to do them as not use it.

HOW far that little candle throws his beams!
    So shines a good deed in a naughty world.
Heaven doth with us as we with torches do;
Not light them for themselves; for if our virtues
Did not go forth of us, 'twere all alike
As if we had them not.

William Shakespeare

201

YOU MAY COUNT THAT DAY

A class of little settlement girls besought Mrs. George Herbert Palmer, one insufferable summer morning, to tell them how to be happy. "I'll give you three rules," she said, "and you must keep them every day for a week. First, commit something good to memory each day. Three or four words will do, just a pretty bit of poem, or a Bible verse. Do you understand?" A girl jumped up. "I know; you want us to learn something we'd be glad to remember if we went blind." Mrs. Palmer was relieved; these children understood. She gave the three rules— memorize something good each day, see something beautiful each day, do something helpful each day. When the children reported at the end of the week, not a single day had any of them lost. But hard put to it to obey her? Indeed they had been. One girl, kept for 24 hours within squalid home-walls by a rain, had nevertheless seen two beautiful things—a sparrow taking a bath in the gutter, and a gleam of sunlight on a baby's hair.

IF you sit down at set of sun
And count the acts that you have done,
    And, counting, find
One self-denying deed, one word
That eased the heart of him who heard—
    One glance most kind,
That fell like sunshine where it went—
Then you may count that day well spent.

But if, through all the livelong day,
You've cheered no heart, by yea or nay—
    If, through it all
You've nothing done that you can trace
That brought the sunshine to one face—
    No act most small
That helped some soul and nothing cost—
Then count that day as worse than lost.

George Eliot

SADNESS AND MERRIMENT
(Adapted from "The Merchant of Venice")

In this passage, Antonio states that he is overcome by a sadness he cannot account for. Salarino tells him that the mental attitude is everything; that mirth is as easy as gloom; that nature in her freakishness makes some men laugh at trifles until their eyes become mere slits, yet leaves others dour and unsmiling before jests that would convulse even the venerable Nestor. Gratiano maintains that Antonio is too absorbed in worldly affairs, and that he must not let his spirits grow sluggish or irritable.

ANT. In sooth, I know not why I am so sad:
It wearies me; you say it wearies you;
But how I caught it, found it, or came by it,
What stuff 'tis made of, whereof it is born,
I am to learn.

Salar. Then let's say you are sad
Because you are not merry: and 'twere as easy
For you to laugh and leap, and say you are merry,
Because you are not sad. Now, by two-headed Janus,
Nature hath framed strange fellows in her time:
Some that will evermore peep through their eyes
And laugh like parrots at a bagpiper,
And other of such vinegar aspect
That they'll not show their teeth in a way of smile,
Though Nestor swear the jest be laughable.

Gra. You look not well, Signior Antonio;
You have too much respect upon the world;
They lose it that do buy it with much care;
Believe me, you are marvelously changed.

Ant. I hold the world but as the world, Gratiano,
A stage where every man must play a part,
And mine a sad one.

> *Gra.*   Let me play the fool:
> With mirth and laughter let old wrinkles come,
> And let my liver rather heat with wine
> Than my heart cool with mortifying groans.
> Why should a man whose blood is warm within
> Sit like his grandsire cut in alabaster?
> Sleep when he wakes, and creep into a jaundice
> By being peevish? Fare ye well awhile:
> I'll end my exhortation after dinner.
>
> *William Shakespeare*

APPRECIATION

LIFE'S a bully good game with its kicks and cuffs;
  Some smile, some laugh, some bluff;
Some carry a load too heavy to bear
  While some push on with never a care,
But the load will seldom heavy be
  When I appreciate you and you appreciate me.

He who lives by the side of the road
  And helps to bear his brother's load
May seem to travel lone and long
  While the world goes by with a merry song,
But the heart grows warm and sorrows flee
  When I appreciate you and you appreciate me.

When I appreciate you and you appreciate me,
  The road seems short to victory;
It buoys one up and calls "Come on,"
  And days grow brighter with the dawn;
There is no doubt or mystery
  When I appreciate you and you appreciate me.

It's the greatest thought in heaven or earth—
  It helps us know our fellow's worth;

There'd be no wars or bitterness,
   No fear, no hate, no grasping; yes,
It makes work play, and the careworn free
   When I appreciate you and you appreciate me

William Judson Kibby

KEEP SWEET

Even the direst catastrophes may be softened by our attitude to them. Charles II said to those who had gathered about his deathbed: "You'll pardon any little lapses, gentlemen. I've never done this thing before."

DON'T be foolish and get sour when things don't just
   come your way—
Don't you be a pampered baby and declare, "Now I won't play!"
   Just go grinning on and bear it;
   Have you heartache? Millions share it,
   If you earn a crown, you'll wear it—
      Keep sweet.

Don't go handing out your troubles to your busy fellow-
   men—
If you whine around they'll try to keep from meeting you
   again;
   Don't declare the world's "agin" you,
   Don't let pessimism win you,
   Prove there's lots of good stuff in you—
      Keep sweet.

If your dearest hopes seem blighted and despair looms into view,
Set your jaw and whisper grimly, "Though they're false, yet
   I'll be true."
   Never let your heart grow bitter;
   With your lips to Hope's transmitter,
   Hear Love's songbirds bravely twitter,
      "Keep sweet."

Bless your heart, this world's a good one, and will always
    help a man;
Hate, misanthropy, and malice have no place in Nature's plan.
  Help your brother there who's sighing,
  Keep his flag or courage flying;
  Help him try—'twill keep you trying—
      Keep sweet.

Strickland W. Gillilan

MORALITY

We can't always, even when accomplishing, have the ardor of accomplishment; we can only hold to the purpose formed in more inspired hours. After a work is finished, even though it be a good work that our final judgment will approve, we are likely to be oppressed for a time by the anxieties we have passed through; the comfort of effort has left us, and we recall our dreams, our intentions, beside which our actual achievement seems small. In such moments we should remember that just after the delivery of the Gettysburg Address Lincoln believed it an utter failure. Yet the address was a masterpiece of commemorative oratory.

WE cannot kindle when we will
    The fire which in the heart resides;
The spirit bloweth and is still,
In mystery our soul abides.
    But tasks in hours of insight will'd
    Can be through hours of gloom fulfill'd.

With aching hands and bleeding feet
We dig and heap, lay stone on stone;
We bear the burden and the heat
Of the long day and wish 'twere done.
    Not till the hours of light return,
    All we have built do we discern.

Matthew Arnold

A HYMN TO HAPPINESS

A man who owed Artemus Ward two hundred dollars fell into such hard circumstances that Artemus offered to knock off half the debt. "I won't let you outdo me in generosity," said the man; "I'll knock off the other half." Similarly, when we resolve to live down our cases of gloom, fate comes to our aid and removes most of them altogether.

L ET us smile along together,
   Be the weather
    What it may.
Through the waste and wealth of hours,
Plucking flowers
    By the way.
Fragrance from the meadows blowing,
Naught of heat or hatred knowing,
Kindness seeking, kindness sowing,
    Not tomorrow, but today.

Let us sing along, beguiling
Grief to smiling
    In the song.
With the promises of heaven
Let us leaven
    The day long,
Gilding all the duller seemings
With the roselight of our dreamings,
Splashing clouds with sunlight's gleamings,
    Here and there and all along.

Let us live along, the sorrow
Of tomorrow
    Never heed.
In the pages of the present
What is pleasant
    Only read.

Bells but pealing, never knelling,
Hearts with gladness ever swelling,
Tides of charity upwelling
    In our every dream and deed.

Let us hope along together,
Be the weather
    What it may,
Where the sunlight glad is shining,
Not repining
    By the way.
Seek to add our meed and measure
To the old Earth's joy and treasure,
Quaff the crystal cup of pleasure,
    Not tomorrow, but today.

James W. Foley

OPPORTUNITY

Procrastination is not only the thief of time; it also is the grave of opportunity.

IN an old city by the storied shores
Where the bright summit of Olympus soars,
A cryptic statue mounted towards the light—
Heel-winged, tip-toed, and poised for instant flight.

"O statue, tell your name," a traveler cried,
And solemnly the marble lips replied:
"Men call me Opportunity: I lift
My winged feet from earth to show how swift
My flight, how short my stay—
How Fate is ever waiting on the way."

"But why that tossing ringlet on your brow?"
"That men may seize me any moment: Now,
NOW is my other name: Today my date:
O traveler, tomorrow is too late!"

Edwin Markham

TO A YOUNG MAN

"Jones write a book! Impossible! I knew his father." This attitude towards a distinction of any sort, whether in authorship or in the field of action is characteristic of many of us. We think transcendent ability is entirely above and apart from the things of ordinary life. Yet genius itself has been defined as common sense in an uncommon degree. The great men are human. Shakespeare remembered this when he said, "I think the king is but a man as I am." We should take heart at the thought that since the great are like us, we may develop ourselves until we are like them.

THE great were once as you.
    They whom men magnify today
Once groped and blundered on life's way,
Were fearful of themselves, and thought
By magic was men's greatness wrought.
They feared to try what they could do;
Yet Fame hath crowned with her success
The selfsame gifts that you possess.

The great were young as you,
Dreaming the very dreams you hold,
Longing yet fearing to be bold,
Doubting that they themselves possessed
The strength and skill for every test,
Uncertain of the truths they knew,
Not sure that they could stand to fate
With all the courage of the great.

Then came a day when they
Their first bold venture made,
Scorning to cry for aid.
They darted to stand to fight alone,
Took up the gauntlet life had thrown,
Charged full-front to the fray,
Mastered their fear of self, and then
Learned that our great men are but men.

Oh, Youth, go forth and do!
You, too, to fame may rise;
You can be strong and wise.
Stand up to life and play the man—
You can if you'll but think you can;
The great were once as you.
You envy them their proud success?
'Twas won with gifts that you possess.

Edgar A. Guest

SLOGAN

Some men want ideal conditions with pay in advance before they will work. But the world does not want such men and has little place for them.

D ON'T prate about what is your right,
But bare your fists and show your might;
Life is another man to fight
Catch as catch can.

Don't talk of Life as scurvy Fate,
Who gave you favors just too late,
Or Luck who threw you smiles for bait
Before he ran.

Don't whine and wish that you were dead,
But wrestle for your daily bread,
And afterward let it be said
"He was a man."

Jane M'Lean

SMILES

Smiles bring out the latent energies within us, as water reveals the bright colors in the stone it flows over.

SMILE a little, smile a little,
   As you go along,
Not alone when life is pleasant
   But when things go wrong.
Care delights to see you frowning,
   Loves to hear you sigh;
Turn a smiling face upon her,
   Quick the dame will fly.

Smile a little, smile a little,
   All along the road;
Every life must have its burden,
   Every heart its load.
Why sit down in gloom and darkness,
   With your grief to sup?
As you drink Fate's bitter tonic
   Smile across the cup.

Smile upon the troubled pilgrims
   Whom you pass and meet;
Frowns are the thorns, and smiles are the blossoms
   Oft for weary feet.
Do not make the way seem harder
   By a sullen face,
Smile a little, smile a little,
   Brighten up the place.

Smile upon your undone labor;
   Not for one who grieves
O'er his task, waits wealth or glory;
   He who smiles achieves.
Though you meet with loss and sorrow
   In the passing years,
Smile a little, smile a little,
   Even through your tears.

Ella Wheeler Wilcox

SIT DOWN, SAD SOUL

"A watched pot never boils." Though the pot be the pot of happiness, the proverb still holds true.

SIT down, sad soul, and count
   The moments flying:
Come—tell the sweet amount
   That's lost by sighing!
How many smiles?—a score?
Then laugh, and count no more;
   For day is dying.

Lie down, sad soul, and sleep,
   And no more measure
The flight of Time, nor weep
   The loss of leisure;
But there, by this lone stream,
Lie down with us and dream
   Of starry treasure.

We dream: do thou the same:
   We love—forever;
We laugh; yet few we shame,
   The gentle, never.
Stay, then, till Sorrow dies;
Then—hope and happy skies
   Are thine forever!

Bryan Waller Procter

SONG OF ENDEAVOR

Don Quixote discovered that there are no eggs in last year's birds' nests. Many of us waste our time in regrets for the past, without seeming to perceive that hope lies only in endeavor for the future.

'TIS not by wishing that we gain the prize,
    Nor yet by ruing,
But from our falling, learning how to rise,
    And tireless doing.

The idols are broken, nor our tears and sighs,
    May yet restore them.
Regret is only for fools; the wise
    Look but before them.

Nor ever yet Success was wooed with tears;
    To notes of gladness
Alone the fickle goddess turns her ears,
    She hears not sadness.

The heart thrives not in the dull rain and mist
    Of gloomy pining.
The sweetest flowers are the flowers sun-kissed,
    Where glad light's shining.

Look not behind thee; there is only dust
    And vain regretting.
The lost tide ebbs; in the next flood thou must
    Learn, by forgetting.

For the lost chances be ye not distressed
    To endless weeping;
Be not the thrush that o'er the empty nest
    Is vigil keeping.

But in new efforts our regrets today
    To stillness whiling,
Let us in some pure purpose find the way
    To future smiling.

                                James W. Foley

KEEP A-GOIN'!

Some men fail and quit. Some succeed and quit. The wise refuse to quit, whether they fail or succeed.

E F you strike a thorn or rose,
    Keep a-goin'!
Ef it hails, or ef it snows,
    Keep a-goin'!
'Taint no use to sit an' whine,
When the fish ain't on yer line;
Bait yer hook an' keep a-tryin'—
    Keep a-goin'!

When the weather kills yer crop,
    Keep a-goin'!
When you tumble from the top,
    Keep a-goin'!
S'pose you're out of every dime,
Bein' so ain't any crime;
Tell the world you're feelin' prime—
    Keep a-goin'!

When it looks like all is up,
    Keep a-goin'!
Drain the sweetness from the cup,
    Keep a-goin'!
See the wild birds on the wing,
Hear the bells that sweetly ring,
When you feel like sighin' sing—
    Keep a-goin'!

Frank L. Stanton

WHEN EARTH'S LAST PICTURE IS PAINTED

What is it that a human being wants? Most of us have something that we like to do more than anything else. We are not free to do it as we wish. We are handicapped by the need to earn a living, by physical weariness, by the carpings and scoffs of the envious, by the limited time we have at our disposal. But underneath all this is the spirit of work—the desire to take up our task for its own sake alone, to give our whole selves to it, to carry it through, not in some partial way but in accordance with the fullness of our dream. We want to be free from distractions and interruptions; if we are driven at all, we want it to be by our own inner promptings, not by obligation or necessity. Of course, these favorable, these ideal conditions belong to heaven, not to earth. Kipling here explains what they will mean to the artist, the painter; but in doing so he expresses the longings of the true workman of whatsoever sort—he sums up the true spirit of work.

WHEN Earth's last picture is painted and the tubes are
          twisted and dried,
When the oldest colors have faded, and the youngest
          critic has died,
We shall rest, and, faith, we shall need it—lie down for
          an aeon or two,
Till the Master of All Good Workmen shall set us to
          work anew.

And those that were good will be happy: they shall sit in
          a golden chair;
They shall splash at a ten-league canvas with brushes of
          comets' hair.
They shall find real saints to draw from—Magdalene,
          Peter, and Paul;
They shall work for an age at a sitting and never be
          tired at all!

And only the Master shall praise us, and only the Master
          shall blame;
And no one shall work for money, and no one shall work
          for fame,
But each for the joy of the working, and each, in his
          separate star,
Shall draw the thing as he sees It for the God of Things
          as They are!

                                        Rudyard Kipling

CROSSING THE BAR

Alfred Lord Tennyson requested that this poem be placed at the end of all editions of his poems, and it is a fitting end to this book, for it provides hope in the face of the greatest unknown—Death. The poet, near the end of his life, calmly and bravely says farewell to the physical world. He likens his passing to the ebbing of the tide—a quiet journey to the afterlife.

SUNSET and evening star,
   And one clear call for me!
And may there be no moaning of the bar,
   When I put out to sea,

But such a tide as moving seems asleep,
   Too full for sound and foam,
When that which drew from out the boundless deep
   Turns again home.

Twilight and evening bell,
   And after that the dark!
And may there be no sadness of farewell,
   When I embark;

For though from out our bourne of Time and Place
   The flood may bear me far,
I hope to see my Pilot face to face
   When I have crossed the bar.

Alfred Lord Tennyson

INDEX BY AUTHORS

A

Adams, St. Clair. Born in Arkansas, 1883. University education; European travel; resided at one time or another in nearly all sections of America.

Alexander, Griffith. Born in Liverpool, Eng., Jan. 15, 1868. Educated in public schools; came to the United States 1887; worked at newspapers in a variety of capacities; president of the American Press Humorists.

Appleton, Everard Jack. Born in Charleston, W. Va., March 24, 1872. Died in 1931. Very little schooling but had advantages of home literary influences and a good library; at 17 went into newspaper work in his hometown; later, in Cincinnati, worked on the daily Tribune, the Commercial Gazette, and the Times-Star. For five years, he wrote a daily column of verse and humor; besides his newspaper work, he wrote more than 150 stories, hundreds of poems, many songs, and innumerable jokes, jingles, cards, etc. Author of two books of poetry. His health broke down, and for a number of years he was a chronic invalid but one who retained a cheerful outlook.

Arnold, Matthew. Born in Laleham, Middlesex, Eng., Dec. 24, 1822; died in Liverpool, April 15, 1888. Educated at Winchester, Rugby, and Oxford. Became Lord Lansdowne's secretary 1847; became inspector of schools 1851; appointed Professor of Poetry at Oxford 1857; continental tours to inspect foreign educational systems 1859 and 1865; assigned a pension of 250 pounds by Gladstone 1883; lecture trips to America 1883 and 1886; retired as inspector of schools 1886. An important English poet.

B

Bangs, John Kendrick. Born in Yonkers, N.Y., May 27, 1862; died Jan. 21, 1922. Received Bachelor of Philosophy degree from Columbia 1883; associate editor of Life magazine 1884-8; served in various editorial capacities for Harper's magazine, Harper's Weekly, and the Metropolitan magazine. He authored a number of books.

Barbauld, Anna Letitia Aiken. Born in Kibworth-Harcourt, Leicestershire, Eng., June 20, 1743; died March 9, 1825. Poet and essayist.

Benét, William Rose. Born in Fort Hamilton, New York Harbor, Feb. 2, 1886.

Died in 1950. Graduated from Albany, N.Y., Academy 1904; Bachelor of Philosophy degree from Sheffield Scientific School of Yale University 1907. Reader for Century magazine 1907-11; assistant editor of that publication 1911-14. 2nd lieutenant U.S. Air Service 1914-18. Assistant editor of the Nation's Business 1919. Author of several books.

Benjamin, Park. Born in Demerara, British Guiana, Aug. 14, 1809; died in New York City, Sept. 12, 1864. Connected with various periodicals.

Binns, Henry Bryan. No biographical information available.

Bradford, Gamaliel. Born in Boston, Mass., Oct. 9, 1863. Died in 1932. Privately tutored until 1882; entered Harvard College 1882 but was obliged to leave almost immediately because of ill health. Contributor of essays and poems to various magazines; had remarkable insight into the characters of historical figures. Published numerous books.

Braley, Berton. Born in Madison, Wis., Jan. 29, 1882. Died in 1966. Graduated from the University of Wisconsin 1905; reporter on the Butte, Mont., Inter Mountain newspaper 1905-6; later with the Butte Evening News and the Billings, Mont., Gazette. He was with the New York Evening Mail 1909; associate editor of Puck 1910; freelance writer from 1910; special correspondent in Northern Europe 1915-16; in France, England, and Germany 1918-19. Numerous books published.

Branch, Anna Hempstead. Born in New London, Conn. Birth date unknown. Died in 1937. Graduated at Adelphi Academy, Brooklyn, 1893, from Smith College 1897, and from the American Academy of Dramatic Art, New York, 1900. Numerous books.

Browning, Elizabeth Barrett. Born in Coxhoe Hall, Durham, Eng., March 6, 1806; died in Florence, Italy, June 30, 1861. A semi-invalid all her life. Married Robert Browning 1846 and resided in Italy for the remainder of her life.

Browning, Robert. Born in Camberwell, Eng., May 7, 1812; died in Venice, Italy, Dec. 12, 1889. Educated at home and at London University; well trained in music. Travel in Russia 1833; considered diplomatic career; trip to Italy 1838; married Elizabeth Barrett 1846, and during her lifetime he resided chiefly in Florence, Italy. After her death, he lived in London and Venice. An important English poet.

Burns, Robert. Born in Alloway, near Ayr, Scotland, Jan. 25, 1759; died at Dumfries, Scotland, July 21, 1796. Received little education; drudgery on a farm at Mt. Oliphant 1766-77; on a farm at Lochlea 1777-84, during which time there was a period of loose living and bad companionship; at the death of his father he and his brother Gilbert rented Mossgiel farm near Mauchline, where many of his best poems were written; winter of 1786-7 he visited Edinburgh and was received into the best society; winter of 1787-8 revisited Edinburg but rather coolly received by Edinburg society; 1788 married Jean Armour, by whom he had previously had several children. Took farm at Ellisland 1788; became an excise officer 1789. Later years characterized by depression and poverty. Wrote many of the most popular songs in the English language.

Byron, Lord (George Gordon Byron). Born in London, Jan. 22, 1788; died in Missolonghi, Greece, April 19, 1824, and buried in parish church at Hucknell near Newstead. Born with a deformed foot; much petted as a child; inherited title and estate at death of his granduncle, William, fifth Lord Byron, 1798. Studied at Harrow and at Cambridge University, receiving M.A. degree 1808. Traveled in Portugal, Spain, Greece, and Turkey 1809-11. In 1815 married Anna Milbanke, who left him 1816. In 1816 met Miss Clairmont at Geneva, who bore him an illegitimate daughter, Allegra, 1817; in 1819 met Teresa, Countess Guiccioli, at Venice, and remained with her during his stay in Italy. Joined the Greek insurgents 1823 and died of a fever in their cause of freedom from the Turks. A major English poet.

C

Carlyle, Thomas. Born in Ecclefechan, Dumfriesshire, Scotland, Dec. 4, 1795; died at Chelsea, London, Feb. 4, 1881. Educated at Annan Grammar School and Edinburgh University; mathematical tutor at Annan 1814; teacher at Kirkcaldy 1816; went to Edinburgh to study law 1819; tutor in Buller family 1822-4; married Jane Welsh 1826; lived successively at Comely Bank, Edinburgh, and Craigenputtoch 1828-34; moved to Chelsea 1834; and remained there the rest of his life. Elected Lord Rector of Edinburgh University 1865. A major English writer. Well-known for his essays.

Clough, Arthur Hugh. Born in Liverpool, Eng., Jan. 1, 1819; died at Florence, Italy, Nov. 13, 1861. Went to school at Rugby and Oxford; accepted headship of University Hall, London, 1849; came to America 1852; health began to fail 1859.

Coates, Florence Earle. Born in Philadelphia, Penn. (date unknown) Died in 1927. Educated at private schools and at the Convent of the Sacred Heart, France; studied also at Brussels. President of the Browning Society of Philadelphia 1895-1903 and 1907-8; a founder of the Contemporary Club,

Philadelphia, 1886; member of the Society of Mayflower Descendants and Colonial Dames of America.

Cooke, Edmund Vance. Born in Port Dover, Canada, June 5, 1866. Died in 1932. Educated principally at common schools. He began to give lectures in 1893 and for a number of years was a very popular public figure. Frequent contributor of poems, stories, and articles to leading magazines. His poem, "How Did You Die?" attained nationwide popularity.

Crosby, Ernest Howard. Born in New York City, Nov. 4, 1856; died there Jan. 3, 1907. Graduated from University of New York 1876 and from Columbia Law School 1878; lawyer in New York 1878-89; judge of international court at Alexandria, Egypt, 1889-94; returned to New York 1894 and became interested in social reform.

D

Dekker, Thomas. Born in London about 1570; died about 1641. Little is know of his life; imprisoned several times; had literary quarrels with Ben Jonson. Well-known English dramatist. Lived in the great period of the English drama (the age of Shakespeare); wrote many of his plays in collaboration with other writers of the period.

Drake, Joseph Rodman. Born in New York City, Aug. 7, 1795; died there Sept. 21, 1820.

E

Eliot, George (Mary Ann Evans Lewes Cross). Born in Arbury Farm, Warwickshire, Eng., Nov. 22, 1819; died at Chelsea, London, Dec. 22, 1880. Educated at Nuneaton and Coventry; assistant editor for the Westminster Review 1851-3. Lived with George Henry Lewes from 1854 until his death in 1878; married John Walter Cross in 1880. Wrote such well-known English novels as "Silas Marner," "Daniel Deronda," and "Middlemarch."

Emerson, Ralph Waldo. Born in Boston, Mass., May 25, 1803; died at Concord, Mass., April 27, 1882. Graduated from Harvard College 1821, working his way; taught school; began to study for the ministry 1823; licensed to preach 1826; trip to the South for his health 1827-8; Unitarian minister in Boston 1829-32; European travel 1832-3; settled at Concord 1834; lectured extensively for more than 30 years. A leader of the American Transcendentalists, a New England group that included Thoreau and which emphasized the intuitive and spiritual above the empirical. Contributed to the Dial magazine 1840-4; visited Europe 1847-8 and 1872-3. Lectured at Harvard 1868-70. An important American essayist.

F

Foley, James William. Born in St. Louis, Mo., Feb. 4, 1874. Died in 1939. Educated at the University of South Dakota. Member of the Masonic Order and Past Grand Master of Masons. Had early ranch experience; knew Theodore Roosevelt during his ranching days. Began newspaper work on the Bismarck, N. Dak., Tribune 1892. During WW II, he served 17 months in army camps as an entertainer and inspirational lecturer, traveling 50,000 miles and addressing some 250,000 men. Afterward, he worked on the Evening Post in Pasadena, Calif. He also lectured and wrote verse, humorous sketches, and plays.

Foss, Sam Walter. Born in Candia, N.H., June 19, 1858; died in 1911. Graduated from Brown University 1882; editor 1883-93; general writer 1893-8; librarian at Somerville, Mass., from 1898; lecturer and reader of his own poems. Published a number of books.

Fowler, Ellen Thorneycroft. (The Honorable Mrs. Alfred Felkin). Elder daughter of 1st Viscount Wolverhampton; married to Alfred Laurence Felkin 1903. Published a number of books.

G

Garrison, Theodosia. Born in Newark, N.J., 1874. Died in 1944. Educated at private schools in Newark. Married Joseph Garrison of Newark 1898; married Frederick J. Faulks of Newark 1911. Several books.

Gates, Ellen M. Huntington. Born in Torrington, Conn., 1834; died in New York City, Oct. 12, 1920. Schooling in Hamilton, N.Y. Several books.

Gillilan, Strickland W. Born in Jackson, Ohio, Oct. 9, 1869. Died in 1954. Attended Ohio University to junior year; began newspaper work on the Jackson, Ohio, Herald 1887; then on the staffs of many newspapers and magazines in various capacities. Writer of humorous verse; popular lecturer. Several books.

Gilman, Charlotte Perkins. Born in Hartford, Conn., June 3, 1860. Died in 1935. Excellent home instruction; school attendance scant; real education reading and thinking, mainly in natural science, history, and sociology. Writer and lecturer on humanitarian topics, especially along lines of educational legal advancement. The Forerunner, a monthly magazine, entirely written by her, published for seven years from 1910. Numerous publications.

Glaenzer, Richard Butler. Born in Paris, France, Dec. 15, 1876. Died in 1937. Educated at the Hill School and Yale. Interior decorator, poet, and essayist. Wrote movie scripts in Hollywood.

Goethe, Johann Wolfgang Von. Born in Frankfort-on-the-Main, Germany, August 28, 1749; died at Weimar, Mar. 22, 1832. Famous poet, dramatist, and prose writer. Among his well-known works are "The Sorrows of Young Werther," "Wilhelm Meister," "Hermann and Dorothea," and "Faust."

Gray, Thomas. Born in London, Dec. 26, 1716; died in Cambridge, July 30, 1771. Educated at Eton and Cambridge; went with Horace Walpole on trip to Continent 1739-41; became professor of modern history at Cambridge 1768 but did not teach. A man singularly retiring and shy throughout his life. Among his well-known poems are "Ode on a Distant Prospect of Eton College," "Elegy Written in a Country Churchyard," "The Progress of Poetry," "The Bard," "The Fatal Sisters," and "The Descent of Odin."

Guest, Edgar Albert. Born in Birmingham, Eng., Aug. 20, 1881. Died in 1959. Brought to the United States 1891; educated in grammar and high schools of Detroit, Mich. Worked for the Detroit Free Press; syndicated a daily poem in several hundred newspapers. Published many books of verse. At one time, one of the most popular poets in America but thought too simple by literary pundits.

H

Henley, William Ernest. Born at Gloucester, Eng., Aug. 23, 1849; died July 11, 1903. Educated at the Crypt Grammar School at Gloucester. Afflicted with physical infirmity; in hospital at Edinburgh 1874—an experience that led to material for his book "Hospital Sketches." Went to London 1877; edited art magazine called London 1882-6; edited the Scots Observer, which became the National Observer, 1888-93; edited the New Review 1893-8. Besides three plays that he wrote in collaboration with Robert Louis Stevenson, he also was the author of several books.

Herbert, George. Born in Montgomery Castle, Wales, Apr. 3, 1593; died in Bemerton, near Salisbury, Eng., Feb., 1633. Graduated from Cambridge 1613; took M.A. degree 1616. He was in high favor at court; appointed by the King as rector to Bemerton Church in 1630, and there he wrote the religious poems for which he is remembered.

Holland, Josiah Gilbert. Born in Belchertown, Mass., July 24, 1819; died in New York City, Oct. 21, 1881. Editor of the Springfield Republican 1849-66; editor-in-chief of Scribner's Monthly (which later became Century Magazine).

Holmes, Oliver Wendell. Born in Cambridge, Mass., Aug. 29, 1809; died there Oct. 7, 1894. Physician; professor of anatomy and physiology in the Harvard University Medical School 1847-82. Published three novels and became well known as a poet.

Hunt, James Henry Leigh. Born at Southgate, Eng., Oct. 19, 1784; died at Putney, Eng., Aug. 28, 1859. Imprisoned for radical political views; writer of popular poems and essays.

I

Ingalls, John James. Born in Middleton, Mass., Dec. 29, 1833; died in Las Vegas, New Mexico., Aug. 16, 1900. Educated at Williams College; admitted to the bar 1857; moved to Kansas; member of the Kansas Senate 1861; U.S. senator from Kansas 1873-91.

J

Jonson, Ben. Born in Westminster, Eng., about 1573; died Aug. 6, 1637. Went to school at St. Martin's-in-the-Fields and Westminster. Shakespeare played one of the roles in his comedy "Every Man in His Humour" 1598. He went to France as the tutor of the son of Sir Walter Raleigh 1613; was in the favor of the court, from which he received a pension. Attacked with palsy 1626, and later with edema, and confined to his bed most of his later years. His other well-known plays include "Epicene," "The Alchemist," "Volpone," "Bartholomew Fair," and Cataline"; author of the lyric "Drink to Me Only with Thine Eyes" and a volume of criticism, "Timber."

K

Keats, John. Born in London, Oct. 29, 1795; died in Rome, Feb. 23, 1821. Went to Enfield School; apprenticed to a druggist 1811-15; student in London hospitals 1815-17; passed examination at Apothecaries Hall 1816 but never practiced. Walking trip to Scotland 1818; his health rapidly failed, and he sailed to Naples in Sept. 1820, then went to Rome where, until his death, he was attended by his friend Severn. Though he lived only 26 years, Keats created some of the best-known poems in English, including "On First Looking into Chapman's Homer," "Endymion," "The Eve of St. Agnes," "Isabella," "La

Belle Dame Sans Merci," "Ode to Psyche," "Ode to a Grecian Urn," "Ode to a Nightingale," "Ode on Melancholy," "Lamia," "Ode to Autumn," and "Hyperion."

Kibby, William Judson. Born in Knoxville, Tenn., March 12, 1876. Educated in Knoxville public schools; graduate of the Sheldon School. Character analyst and industrial psychologist; newspaper and magazine contributor. President of the Lion's Club of New York; thirty-second degree Mason.

King, Benjamin Franklin, Jr. Born in St. Joseph, Mich., March 17, 1857; died in Bowling Green, Ky., April 7, 1894. At an early age showed a remarkable talent in music; a public entertainer on the piano and reciter of his own verse.

Kipling, Rudyard. Born in Bombay, India, Dec. 30, 1865. Died in 1936. Educated in England at United Service College; returned to India 1880; assistant editor of Civil and Military Gazette 1882-89; returned to England 1889; resided in the United States for several years; traveled in Japan and Australia. Received the Nobel Prize for Literature 1907; honorary degrees from McGill University, Durham, Oxford, and Cambridge. Among his many books are "Departmental Ditties," "Plain Tales from the Hills," "Under the Deodars," "Phantom 'Rickshaw," "Wee Willie Winkle," "Life's Handicap," "The Light That Failed," "Barrack-Room Ballads," "The Jungle Book," "The Second Jungle Book," "The Seven Seas," "Captains Courageous," "The Day's Work," "Kim," "Just So Stories," "Puck of Pook's Hill," "Actions and Reactions," "Rewards and Fairies," "Fringes of the Fleet," and "Sea Warfare."

Kiser, Samuel Ellsworth. Born in Shippenville, Penn., in 1862. Died in 1942. Educated in Pennsylvania and Ohio. Began newspaper work in Cleveland, and from 1900 to 1914 was editorial and special writer for the Chicago Record-Herald. Noted for his humorous sketches, which have been widely syndicated. His poem "Unsubdued" is, like Henley's "Invictus," a portrayal of undaunted courage in the face of defeat. Published a number of books.

Knox, J. Mason. No information could be found.

L

Longfellow, Henry Wadsworth. Born in Portland, Maine, Feb. 27, 1807; died in Cambridge, Mass., March 24, 1882. Graduated from Bowdoin College 1825; traveled in Europe 1826-9; professor of modern languages at Bowdoin 1829-34; again visited Europe 1835-6; professor of modern languages and belles lettres at Harvard College 1836-54; European travel 1869-9. An influential

American poet; best-known poems are "A Psalm of Life," "The Village Blacksmith," "The Wreck of the Hesperus," "The Skeleton in Armor," "The Bridge," "Evangeline," "The Building of the Ship," "Hiawatha," "The Courtship of Miles Standish," and "Tales of a Wayside Inn." He also authored two novels, "Hyperion" and "Kavanagh" and translated Dante's "Divine Comedy."

Lovelace, Richard. Born in Kent, Eng., 1618; died in London, 1658. Educated at Oxford; imprisoned for support of the royalist cause 1642 and 1648; released from prison after the execution of King Charles I, but his estate had been ruined, and he died in poverty.

M

Mackay, Charles. Born in Perth, Eng., March 27, 1814; died in London, Dec. 24, 1889. Editor of the Glasgow Argus 1844-47 and of the Illustrated London News 1852-59; New York correspondent of the London Times.

M'Lean, Jane. No biography available.

Malloch, Douglas. Born in Muskegon, Mich., May 5, 1877. Died in 1938. Common school education; reporter on the Muskegon Daily Chronicle 1886-1903; member of the editorial staff of the American Lumberman in 1903 and associate editor in 1910; contributed verse relating to the forest and lumber camps to various magazines; was called "The Poet of the Woods."

Malone, Walter. Born in De Soto Co., Miss., Feb. 10, 1866; died May 18, 1915. Received the Bachelor of Philosophy degree from the University of Mississippi 1887; practiced law in Memphis, Tenn.; literary work in New York City 1897-1900; then resumed law practice in Memphis; became judge of the second Circuit Court, Shelby Co., Tenn., 1905, and served till his death. Annual exercises were held in the Capleville schools in his honor.

Markham, Edwin. Born in Oregon City, Ore., April 23, 1852. Died in 1940. Went to California 1857; worked at farming and blacksmithing and herded cattle and sheep during his boyhood. Educated at San Jose Normal School and two Western colleges; special student in ancient and modern literature and Christian sociology; principal and superintendent of schools in California until 1899. He is a distinguished American poet. His poem "The Man with the Hoe" in his first volume of poems is world-famous; it was heralded by many as "the battle cry of the next thousand years." He sounded in his work the note of universal brotherhood and humanitarian interest and was credited with opening a new school of American poetry appealing to the social conscience.

Mason, Walt. Born in Columbus, Ontario, May 4, 1862. Died in 1939. Self-educated. Came to the United States 1880; was connected with the Atchison, Kan., Globe 1885-7; later with, Lincoln, Neb., State Journal; editorial paragrapher of the Washington, Kan., Evening News, 1893; with the Emporia, Kan., Gazette from 1907. Wrote a daily prose poem that was syndicated in more than two hundred newspapers and was believed to have the largest audience of any living writer.

Miller, Joaquin. Born in Indiana, Nov. 11, 1841; died Feb. 17, 1913. Went to Oregon 1854; was afterwards a miner in California; studied law; was a judge in Grand County, Oregon, 1866-7. For a while, he was a journalist in Washington, D.C.; returned to California 1887. He was the author of various books of verse and was called "The Poet of the Sierras."

Milton, John. Born in London, Dec. 9, 1608; died there Nov. 8, 1674. Attended St. Paul's School; at Cambridge 1625-32. At Horton, writing and studying, 1632-38. In 1638 went to Italy; met Galileo in Florence. During the great English Civil War wrote pamphlets against the Royalists; was made Latin Secretary to the new Commonwealth 1649; became totally blind 1652. Until his third marriage in 1663, his domestic life was an unhappy one, no doubt exacerbated by three undutiful daughters. He is a major English language poet, best known for his prodigious work, "Paradise Lost."

Morgan, Angela. Born in Washington, D.C. Date of birth unknown. Died in 1957. Educated under private tutors and at public schools; took special work at Columbia University. Began early as a newspaper writer, first the Chicago American, then with the Chicago Journal and New York and Boston papers. She was a member of the Poetry Society of America. She was known as one of the most eloquent public readers; was a delegate to the Congress of Women at the Hague 1915, at which she read her poem "Battle Cry of the Mothers." She wrote several novels as well as poetry.

Morris, Joseph. Born in Ohio 1889. Died in 1947. College and university education; professor of English and lecturer on literary subjects; newspaper and magazine contributor; connected with publishing houses from 1917 in various editorial capacities.

N

Neihardt, John Gneisenau. Born near Sharpsburg, Ill., Jan. 8, 1881. Died in

1973. Completed the scientific course at the Nebraska Normal College 1897; received the degree of Litt.D. from the University of Nebraska 1917. Declared Poet Laureate of Nebraska by the Legislature, April 1921, in recognition of the significance of his American epic cycle poem. Winner of the $500 prize by the Poetry Society of America for the best volume of poetry published by an American in 1919. He was a literary critic for the Minneapolis Journal. He wrote books as well as poems, and one that continues to be popular is "Black Elk Speaks."

Nette, Jean. No biographical information available.

Newbolt, Sir Henry. Born in Bilston, Eng., June 6, 1862. Died in 1938. Educated at Oxford; practiced law until 1899; editor of Monthly Review 1900-04; vice president of the Royal Society of Literature; knighted in 1916.

Noyes, Alfred. Born in Staffordshire, Eng., Sept. 16, 1880. Died in 1958. Educated at Oxford; received honorary degree of Litt.D. from Yale 1913; gave the Lowell Lectures in America on "The Sea in English Poetry" 1913; elected to Professorship of Modern Poetry at Princeton 1914; temporarily attached to the Foreign Office 1916. Published a number of books of poetry.

O

O Sheel, Sheamus. Born in New York City, Sept. 19, 1886. Died in 1954. Educated in the New York City grammar and high schools; took special work in English and history at Columbia 1906-08. Member of the Poetry Society of America and the Gaelic Society. Interested in political and civic reforms.

P

Procter, Bryan Waller ("Barry Cornwall"). Born in Leeds, Eng., Nov. 21, 1787; died Oct. 5, 1874. Educated at Harrow; schoolmate of Byron and Sir Robert Peel; called to the bar 1831; commissioner of lunacy 1832-61.

R

Rice, Grantland. Born in Nashville, Tenn., Nov. 1, 1880. Died in 1954. Attended Vanderbilt University. Worked as a sportswriter on the Atlanta Journal; went to New York City 1911. His sports column, "The Spotlight," was said to be more widely syndicated and more widely read than any other writing on sports topics in the United States. A critic said that his sportswriting often reached the height of pure literature. As a writer of homely, simple American verse, he was held by many to be the logical successor to James Whitcomb Riley.

Riley, James Whitcomb. Born in Greenfield, Ind., 1849; died in Indianapolis July 22, 1916. Public school education; received honorary degree of M.A. from Yale 1902; Litt.D. from Wabash College 1903 and from the University of Pennsylvania 1904; LL.D. from Indiana University 1907. Began contributing poems to Indiana papers 1873; known as the "Hoosier Poet"—much of his verse in the middle Western and Hoosier dialect. Wrote numerous books.

Rittenhouse, Jessie Belle. Born in Mt. Morris, N.Y., in 1869. Died in 1948. Graduate of Genesee Wesleyan Seminary, Lima, N.Y.; teacher of Latin and English in a private school in Cairo, Ill., and at Ackley Institute for Girls, Grand Haven, Mich., 1893-4; active in newspaper work and as a reviewer until 1900; contributor to New York Times Review of Books and The Bookman; lecturer on modern poetry in extension courses of Columbia University. She wrote several books of verse.

S

Service, Robert William. Born in Preston, Eng., Jan. 10, 1874. Died in 1958. Educated at Hillhead Public School, Glasgow; served apprenticeship with the Commercial Bank of Scotland, Glasgow; emigrated to Canada and settled on Vancouver Island; for a while engaged in farming; later traveled up and down the Pacific Coast, following many occupations; finally joined the staff of the Canadian Bank of Commerce in Victoria, B.C., 1905; was later transferred to White Horse, Yukon Territory, and then to Dawson; he spent eight years in the Yukon, much of it in travel. In Europe during WW I; in Paris 1921. Received considerable acclaim as a writer of light verse.

Shakespeare, William. Born at Stratford on Avon in 1564; died there in 1616, and buried in Stratford church. Probably attended Stratford Grammar School; married Anne Hathaway, who was eight years his senior, Nov., 1582; a daughter, Susanna, born May 1, 1853; twins, Hamnet and Judith, born 1585. About 1585 went to London and became connected with the theater as an actor, reviser of old plays, etc. His son Hamnet died 1596; his father applied for a coat of arms 1596. Bought New Place at Stratford 1597; coat of arms granted 1599; shareholder in Globe theater 1599. His father died 1601; his daughter Susanna married to John Hall, a physician at Stratford, 1607; his mother died 1608. Retired from theater and returned to Stratford about 1611. His daughter Judith married to Thomas Quinney, a vintner, 1616; his wife died 1623; last descendant, Lady Bernard, died 1670. Folio edition of his plays 1623. Generally acknowledged as the greatest writer in the English language. Characterized by unsurpassed ability in both comedy and tragedy; extraordinary insight into human character; supreme mastery of language. Besides his many plays, he wrote sonnets and two long poems.

Shelley, Percy Bysshe. Born at Field Place, Sussex, Eng., Aug. 4, 1792; drowned off Vireggio, Italy, July 8, 1822. Educated at Eton 1804-10; expelled from Oxford for publication of pamphlet "The Necessity of Atheism" 1811. Married Harriet Westbrook 1811; left her 1814 and went to Switzerland with Mary Godwin; returned to England 1815; received 1,000 pounds a year from his grandfather's estate 1815. Harriet drowned herself 1816, and he formally married Mary the next month. They went to Italy 1818; he drowned on a voyage to welcome poet and critic Leigh Hunt to Italy; his body burned on a funeral pyre in the presence of Lord Byron, Hunt, and prose writer Edward Trelawny. Shelley was one of the three best-known poets of the English Romantic Period in literature, the others being William Wordsworth and John Keats. Though he lived briefly, some of his poems are masterpieces.

Sill, Edward Rowland. Born in Windsor, Conn., 1841; died in Cleveland, Ohio, Feb. 27, 1887. Graduated from Yale 1861; professor of English at University of California 1874-82.

Southwell, Robert. Born about 1561; executed at Tyburn, Eng., Feb. 21, 1595. Educated in Paris; received into the Society of Jesus 1578; returned to England 1586; became chaplain to the Countess of Arundel 1589; betrayed to the authorities 1592; imprisoned for three years before executed.

Stanton, Frank Lebby. Born in Charleston, S.C., Feb. 22, 1857. Died in 1927. Common school education; served apprenticeship as printer; identified with the Atlanta, Ga., press for years, especially with the Atlanta Constitution.

Stevenson, Robert Louis. Born in Edinburgh, Scotland, Nov. 13, 1850; died at Apia, Samoa, Dec. 4, 1894. Early education irregular because of poor health; went to Italy with his parents 1863; at Edinburgh University 1867-73, at first preparing for engineering but later taking up law; admitted to the bar 1875 but never practiced. Various trips to Europe between 1873-79; visited America 1879-80; resided in Switzerland, France, and England 1882-7; came to America again 1887-8; voyages in Pacific 1888-91; at Vailima, Somoa, 1891-94. A perfect example of a man always in poor health yet courageous and optimistic throughout his life. He wrote several books that have become classics, including "Treasure Island," "A Child's Garden of Verse," and "The Strange Case of Dr. Jekyll and Mr. Hyde."

T

Teichner, Miriam. Born in Detroit, Mich., 1888. Educated in public schools there; graduated from Central High School; took special courses in English and economics at the University of Michigan. Member of staff of Detroit News after leaving school, writing a daily column of verse and humor; went to New York City as a special feature writer of the New York Globe 1915; in Germany for the Detroit News and Associated Newspapers, writing of post-war social and economic conditions 1921.

Tennyson, Alfred Lord. Born at Somersby, Lincolnshire, Eng., Aug. 6, 1809; died at Aldworth House, near Haslemere, Surrey, Oct. 6, 1892. Student at Cambridge 1828-31 but did not graduate; trip to the Pyrenees with Arthur Hallam 1832; granted a pension of 200 pounds by Peel 1845; after residing successively at Twickenham and Aldworth, he settled at Farringford, the Isle of Wight, 1853. Became poet laureate of England 1850; raised to the peerage 1884. Considered one of the best of the Victorian poets, Tennyson wrote works that are still widely read and admired, including "The Lady of Shalott," "The Palace of Art," "The Lotus Eaters," "A Dream of Fair Women," "Ulysses," "Locksley Hall," "In Memorium," "Maud," and "Charge of the Light Brigade."

V

Van Dyke, Henry. Born in Germantown, Penn., Nov. 10, 1852. Died in 1933. Graduated from Polytechnical Institute of Brooklyn 1869; A.B. degree from Princeton 1873; M.A. degree from there 1876; graduated from Princeton Theological Seminary 1877; studied at University of Berlin 1877-9; received honorary degrees from Princeton, Harvard, Yale, Union, Wesleyan, Pennsylvania, and Oxford. Pastor of United Congregational Church, Newport, R.I., 1879-82, and of the Brick Presbyterian Church, New York, 1883-1900; U.S. minister to the Netherlands and Luxembourg 1913-17. Author of a number of books on topics ranging from poetry to sermons to criticism.

W

Whittier, John Greenleaf. Born in Haverhill, Mass., Dec. 17, 1807; died in Hampton Falls, N.H., Sept. 7, 1892. Of Quaker ancestry; father a poor farmer; as a boy he injured his health by hard work on the farm. Taught school; attended Haverhill Academy for two terms 1827-8; edited Haverhill Gazette 1830; returned to the farm in broken health 1832. Member of Massachusetts Legislature 1835-6. An ardent opponent of slavery; edited the Pennsylvania Freeman 1838-40; several times attacked by mobs because of his views on slavery. Leading writer for the Washington National Era 1847-57; contributed to the Atlantic Monthly magazine 1857. Some of his well-known poems are "Maud Muller," "The Barefoot Boy," "Barbara Freitchie," "Snow-bound," and "The Eternal Goodness."

Widdemer, Margaret. Born in Doylestown, Penn., in 1880. Educated at home; graduated from the Drexel Institute Library School 1909. Began writing in childhood; her first published poem "The Factories" was widely quoted; married Robert Haven Schauffler 1919. Wrote several books.

Wilcox, Ella Wheeler. Born in Johnston Centre, Wis., 1855; died at her home in Connecticut, Oct. 31, 1919. Educated at the University of Wisconsin. Published many books of poetry and was a well-regarded poet.

Wordsworth, William. Born in Cockermouth, Cumberland, Eng., April 7, 1770; died at Rydal Mount, April 23, 1850. Educated at Hawkshead grammar school and Cambridge University, where he graduated in 1791. Traveled in Europe 1790; in France 1791-92, where he sympathized with the French republicans. Received 900-pound legacy 1795; settled with his sister Dorothy at Racedown, Dorsetshire. To be near Coleridge, he moved to Alfoxden 1797; went to Europe 1798; returned to England 1799 and settled at Grasmere in the lake district; married Mary Hutchison 1802; settled at Allan Bank 1808; moved again to Grasmere 1811. Appointed distributor of stamps 1813 and settled at Rydal Mount; traveled in Scotland 1814 and 1832 and in Europe 1820 and 1837. Given a pension of 300 pounds by Peel 1842; became poet laureate of England 1843. He is considered the major poet of the English Romantic Period and one of the great English poets.

Wotton, Sir Henry. Born at Bocton Malherbe, Kent, Eng., 1568; died at Eton 1639. Educated at Winchester and Oxford; in Europe 1588-95; became secretary of the Earl of Essex 1595; English ambassador to Venice and Germany; became provost of Eton College 1624.